CULTURES OF THE WORLD
Lebanon

Cavendish Square

New York

Published in 2017 by Cavendish Square Publishing, LLC
243 5th Avenue, Suite 136, New York, NY 10016
Copyright © 2017 by Cavendish Square Publishing, LLC

Third Edition

Library of Congress Cataloging-in-Publication Data

Names: Sheehan, Sean, 1951- author. | Latif, Zawiah Abdul, author. | Schmermund, Elizabeth, author.
Title: Lebanon / Sean Sheehan, Zawiah Abdul Latif, and Elizabeth Schmermund.
Other titles: Cultures of the world.
Description: New York : Cavendish Square Publishing, 2017. | Series: Cultures of the world | Includes bibliographical references and index.
Identifiers: LCCN 2016049579 (print) | LCCN 2016057526 (ebook) | ISBN 9781502626127 (library bound) | ISBN 9781502626011 (E-book)
Subjects: LCSH: Lebanon. | Lebanon--Social life and customs.
Classification: LCC DS80 .S53 2017 (print) | LCC DS80 (ebook) | DDC 956.92--dc23
LC record available at https://lccn.loc.gov/2016049579

Editorial Director: David McNamara
Editor: Kristen Susienka
Copy Editor: Nathan Heidelberger
Associate Art Director: Amy Greenan
Designer: Alan Sliwinski
Production Coordinator: Karol Szymczuk
Photo Research: J8 Media

PICTURE CREDITS

Printed in the United States of America

CONTENTS

LEBANON TODAY

THE LEBANESE ARE VERY PROUD OF THEIR HOMELAND, AND FOR good reason. Although Lebanon is a relatively new nation—Greater Lebanon, the predecessor to the modern state, was formed in 1920, and France only recognized Lebanon's independence in 1943—it boasts an ancient and varied culture. The ancient lands of modern-day Lebanon were once at the heart of Phoenician culture. Beginning in the eleventh century BCE, the great Phoenician civilization spread out across the Mediterranean, bringing with them their alphabet—one of the earliest alphabets every developed. In fact, it was the unique location of modern-day Lebanon that allowed the seafaring Phoenicians to spread their culture and their language, and it is what has made Lebanon the crossroads of culture it remains today. Lebanon is a tiny country that is smaller than the US state of Connecticut and holds a population of approximately six million. However, its location on the Mediterranean Sea, across from both southern Europe and North Africa, means that it was the center of an early and important trading route. In fact, many early travelers coming from these areas would pass through Lebanon to go further east in Asia, to Iraq, Iran, and then southern Asia. Lebanon's location molded both its early history and its contemporary culture. Today it remains a melting pot of different cultures, ethnicities, and religions. Safeguarding the country's rich and varied religious heritage, in particular, has been integral to the functioning of the contemporary Lebanese nation.

Lebanon's colonial history also deeply influenced the path modern Lebanon would take. From the sixteenth century to the twentieth century, Lebanon was part of the Ottoman Empire. Over this long history, Lebanon was ruled under vacillating amounts of Ottoman control—sometimes the area experienced tighter control, while other times it was granted relative autonomy. Following World War I, France took Greater Lebanon under the French mandate of Syria and Lebanon. The French influence in Lebanon is still tangible; many Lebanese are fluent in both Arabic and French, and their Arabic is inflected with French words. In fact, Beirut, the capital of Lebanon, was nicknamed the "Paris of the Middle East," as much for its French influences as for its vibrant intellectual and cultural life.

THE NATIONAL PACT

After gaining its independence from France at the end of World War II, Lebanon was enshrined as a multi-confessional state. The National Pact of 1943, upon which the Lebanese government was built, stipulated that the president of the republic must always be a Maronite Catholic, while the prime minister of the republic must always be a Sunni Muslim. Other important government positions were equally divided between religious affiliations so that all of Lebanon's religions were equally represented according to the population at that time. The National Pact also stipulated that Lebanese Christians must accept a politically and culturally Arab Lebanon and not seek Western intervention.

For some time, the National Pact successfully governed the varied population of Lebanon. However, sectarian tension in the region, particularly due to increased fighting between Palestinians (with the aid of other Arab nations) and Israelis in the 1960s, led to radicalization within Lebanon. As Palestinian refugees fleeing violence and discrimination in Israel surged across Lebanon's borders, sectarian tensions within Lebanon flared. Lebanese Christians grew concerned that, with such a large influx of Muslims, they would lose their power and representation in government due to the rapidly changing demographics. Muslims felt that Christians unfairly held too much power in government. There were also tensions between Sunni and Shiite Muslims.

All of this came to a head in the spring of 1975. Clashes between different religiously affiliated militias occurred more frequently until a gunman sped through a Christian suburb in Beirut and fired indiscriminately in front of a church, killing four people, including two members of a Christian militia. The Christian militia soon took revenge, killing twenty-eight Palestinians traveling on a bus. This became widely known as the spark that would start the country's bloody civil war, which would last for fifteen years, until 1990, and would turn into a regional conflict in which Lebanon's neighbors would become implicated as well. Throughout the civil war, retributions were meted out from each militia to its adversaries—and to the civilians who were unfortunately caught up in the fighting. The war would result in over 150,000 deaths and 1 million Lebanese displaced. Beirut—and indeed, the entire country—was decimated. It would take many years—and many more setbacks—to rebuild.

TODAY'S LEBANON

Today, the country is still no stranger to war. Small conflicts have played out in the years since the end of the civil war, and the Syrian civil war, which began in 2011, has unfortunately once again increased tensions within Lebanon between sectarian groups. While the Lebanese have lived through many wars and conflicts, they have rebuilt their country into a successful and powerful nation. In recent years, they have improved human development, women's rights, and democracy in the region. However, the country still has a ways to go with securing rights for its Palestinian population, refugees, and additional rights for women. Political divisions also impeded the election of a president from 2014 until October 2016. Despite these setbacks, the Lebanese have shown over and over again their fortitude, and they will continue to show their strength in the face of adversity.

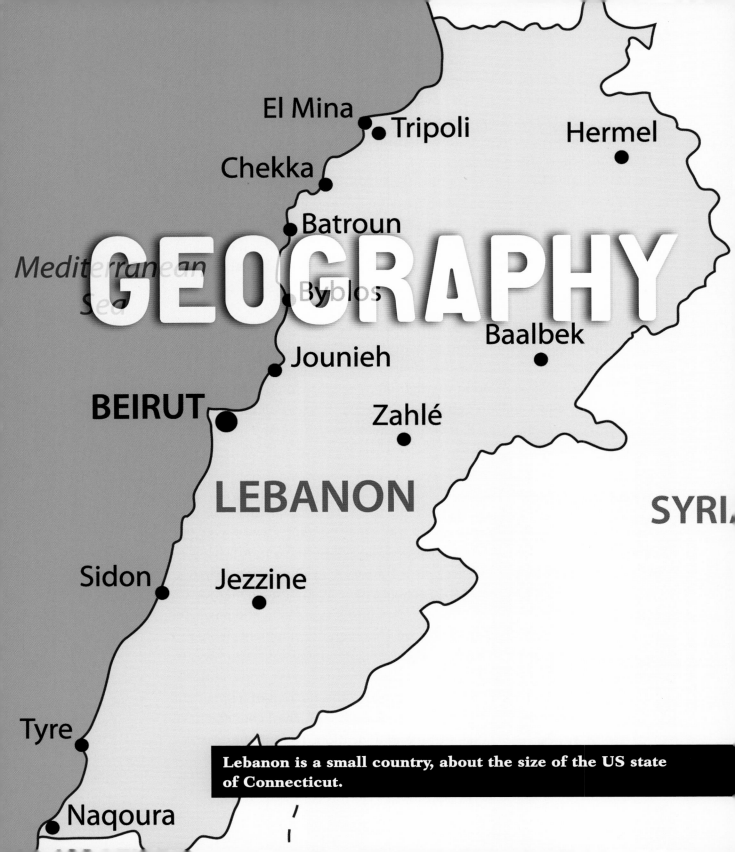

El Mina

Tripoli

Hermel

Chekka

Batroun

Mediterranean Sea

Byblos

Baalbek

Jounieh

BEIRUT

Zahlé

LEBANON

SYRIA

Sidon

Jezzine

Tyre

Lebanon is a small country, about the size of the US state of Connecticut.

Naqoura

ALTHOUGH LEBANON IS A SMALL country, with a total land area of 3,950 square miles (10,230 square kilometers), its varied terrain ranges from rolling mountains to sandy coasts and green woodlands covered by the country's national tree, the cedar. Situated at the eastern edge of the Mediterranean Sea, Lebanon is three times longer than it is wide, which means its coastline stretches for 140 miles (225 kilometers).

It is shaped like a rough rectangle that becomes narrower as you travel north to south. At its narrowest point, Lebanon stretches merely 20 miles (32 km), while its widest point is 55 miles (88 km). Lebanon shares a border with Israel, which shares its southern border; Syria, which stretches to the east and north of the country; and the Mediterranean Sea.

FOUR REGIONS

Lebanon is famous for its notable geographical contrasts, despite its size. Because of its mountainous terrain, the flora and fauna of Lebanon change drastically depending on altitude and location. The mountains that crisscross the country generally run north to south at parallel locations, creating alternating swaths of lowlands and highlands. These areas are typically divided into four distinct regions: the coastal plain, the Lebanon Mountains, the Bekáa Valley, and the Anti-Lebanon Mountains.

COASTAL PLAIN The coastal plain extends along the country's western shoreline. Five of Lebanon's most ancient and historically important cities— Tripoli, Byblos, Beirut, Sidon, and Tyre—developed along this stretch of land aside the Mediterranean. Rocky outcroppings and steep cliffs characterize this area, although just south of Beirut there are many sandy stretches. This narrow region is characterized by warm summers, which provide ideal conditions for growing fruit. In this area, early human civilizations cultivated grains and established communities. The same land is still used for farming; groves of orange and olive trees are a common sight, and bananas and grapes are also cultivated.

LEBANON MOUNTAINS The Lebanon Mountains, called Jabel Lubnan in Arabic, are what gave the country its name. East of the coastal plain, the land rises quickly to form the Lebanon Mountain Range. This mountain range, one

The country's famed cedars dot the Lebanese mountains.

of the country's two highest, extends for almost the entire length of the 110-mile- (170 km) long country parallel to the Mediterranean coast. Lebanon cedars dot the mountains, and when possible, terraces have been cut into the mountains' stone faces to enable the farming of such important crops as olives. These mountains have often been described as "milk white," as snow that can average depths of 13 feet (4 meters) covers the highest peaks at 10,131 feet (3,088 m) tall.

BEKÁA VALLEY The Bekáa Valley, which extends north and east of Beirut, is the country's most important farming region and makes up 40 percent of Lebanon's arable land. This fertile valley provides most of the country's main crops, including tobacco, mulberries, potatoes, citrus fruits, and cotton, mainly because of the temperate rainfall and warm, dry summers experienced in the region. Two rivers originate in the Bekáa Vally: the Orontes, which flows north into Syria, and the Litani, which flows south, eventually winding to the Mediterranean Sea. Aqueducts carry water from these rivers to the crops along the valley.

ANTI-LEBANON RANGE The final geographical region is formed by the interior mountain range that provides a natural border between Syria and Lebanon. These mountains run parallel to the Lebanon Mountains, and their highest crest forms the border with Syria, leaving much of these mountains in Syrian territory. The Anti-Lebanon Mountain Range extends approximately 93 miles (150 km). Due to their high altitude, many of the mountains' peaks are snow-capped year round.

RIVERS

Although there are sixteen rivers in Lebanon, none of them are navigable. This means that they are not deep or wide enough for boats to pass through. Generally, these rivers form in large springs in the Lebanon Mountains and flow down to the waters of the Mediterranean.

There are two main rivers in the Bekáa Valley, the Litani and the Orontes. The Orontes, unusually, flows north into Syria and is nicknamed the Rebel

According to Greek philosopher, historian, and geographer Strabo, Zeus struck the dragon Typhon with a thunderbolt out of the sky, and his falling body created the bed of the Orontes River.

The Litani River is Lebanon's longest and most important river.

River because of its unusual flow direction. The Litani flows south from the city of Baalbek to the Mediterranean Sea just north of Tyre. The Litani is the country's longest and most important river, and the only river in the Near East that does not cross an international boundary.

CLIMATE

Lebanon has a typically Mediterranean climate with long, hot, and dry summers and short, cool, and wet winters. January is typically the coldest month in the country, with temperatures ranging from 41 degrees Fahrenheit (5 degrees Celsius) to 50°F (10°C). In the summer, temperatures can reach 104°F (40°C). November through March is the rainy period, producing 70 percent of the annual rainfall. The most important factor influencing the weather in Lebanon is altitude. Humidity often plagues coastal communities in the summer, and wealthier residents escape to summer homes in the mountains for the cool, fresh mountain breezes.

The mountains also serve as an important physical barrier. Rain-bearing clouds blowing in from the Mediterranean west of Lebanon release moisture when they reach the mountains. In the cool months from November through March, when rains fall in torrents along the coast, the mountains are capped in heavy snowfall. This ensures a supply of water later in the year when the snow melts.

The temperature in the summer months rarely exceeds 90°F (32°C) at sea level, while inland in the mountains the temperature is around 68°F (20°C) in the summer. In the winter the temperature on the coast averages 56°F (13°C). The Bekáa Valley is much drier and cooler than the rest of the country. As such, irrigation is necessary to ensure that there is enough water for the crops. While Beirut receives an average of 36 inches (91 centimeters) of rainfall each year, the Bekáa Valley only sees about 15 inches (38 cm).

The Arabic name for this mountain in the Anti-Lebanon Range, straddling the border with Syria, translates as "Mountain of the Chief." It has three summits; the highest stands at 9,232 feet (2,814 m) above sea level.

For thousands of years, the natural grandeur of Mount Hermon has inspired poets and religious mystics. The remains of a number of ancient temples have been found on its slopes, and it is believed to have been the site of the transfiguration of Jesus Christ.

PLANTS

Lebanon is home to natural wealth of approximately 2,600 different plant species. Of these, common plants and trees include poppy, anemone, oak, fir, pine, and cypress. Olive bushes, fig trees, and grape vines grow abundantly all over the country, while cedar, maple, and other trees grow mostly at higher altitudes. Along the coast, shrubs known as tamarisks grow in salty, low-altitude soil. Tamarisks are known as "salt cedar" and are covered in pink and white flowers for much of the year. Along the rolling hills and mountainsides, wildflowers, including the indigenous Lebanon violet, grow in abundance.

CEDARS OF LEBANON   The Lebanon cedar, or *cedrus libani*, is integrally tied with the country's history and its contemporary identity. In fact, the Lebanon cedar is the national emblem of the country, graces the country's flag, and stands for national pride. Native to the Lebanese Mountains, this aromatic evergreen conifer once grew all over the country and was notably used by ancient Phoenicians to make boats that they then used to explore the world. King Solomon is said to have built his palace from the wood of Lebanon cedars, and the Roman emperor Hadrian created an imperial forest to protect these trees approximately two thousand years ago.

Over the centuries, the cedars have gradually been depleted. They once covered vast areas of the country but are now squeezed into an area of about 5,000 to 7,000 acres (2,000 to 2,800 hectares), a tiny fraction of the country's land area.

The oldest specimens of Lebanese cedars are over two thousand years old.

The most famous stand of cedars still surviving in Lebanon is at Bsharri in the Lebanon Mountains. The Al Shouf Cedar Reserve is located in Chouf, a district under the Mount Lebanon governorate. The oldest and largest specimens of the tree are reported to be over two thousand years old. They are, unfortunately, in a very poor state and show little evidence of propagation. Some visitors make huge cuts on the bark and damage the trees, which are already suffering from receiving insufficient light and water due to overcrowding.

There are plans by environmental organizations to try to save the cedars of Lebanon by reforesting them in new and larger areas of the country. One example is Al Shouf Cedar Reserve, situated southeast of Beirut. It is Lebanon's largest nature reserve, covering 123,550 acres (50,000 ha) of land and boasting six cedar forests. Although there are fewer cedar forests remaining in Lebanon, the tree is still the country's national emblem and is featured on the national flag.

OLIVES Olives are an important crop in Lebanon, grown on narrow-leaved evergreen trees that belong to a botanical family of over thirty different species. The olive plays an important role in Lebanese cuisine and culture, and the oldest olive trees in the world are in Lebanon, where the cool winters and dry summers suit the olives' growth. Today, an estimated thirteen million olive trees form 20 percent of the country's land used for agriculture.

ANIMALS

Due to the small size of the country and its high percentage of cultivated land, few large mammals roam Lebanon's terrain. However, there are many smaller animals of note, including the rock hyrax, a cat-sized mammal that looks like a guinea pig. Surprisingly, the hyrax's closest living relative is the elephant, although its resemblance to the elephant can be seen most clearly in its skeleton, which features tusk-like incisors. Hyraxes typically live among mountain ranges near rock outcroppings in which they shelter.

A number of animals found in Lebanon are threatened with extinction. They include the gray wolf, the mountain gazelle, the imperial eagle, the Mediterranean monk seal, and a species of pelican.

Migratory birds such as cormorants, flamingos, herons, ducks, and pelicans visit the marshes of the Bekáa Valley on their way south in the fall and north in the spring. Birds native to Lebanon include songbirds like the thrush and nightingale.

The cultivation of olive trees is an important part of Lebanon's economy.

LARGEST CITIES

Most of Lebanon's population lives in large towns and cities that dot the Mediterranean coast. These cities were important ports in historical times and feature important historical sites to which tourists flock today. The largest city by population is Lebanon's capital, Beirut, followed by Tripoli, Sidon, and Jounieh.

BEIRUT Beirut is not only the largest city in Lebanon but also one of the largest and most urbanized cities in the Arab world, with a population of approximately 1.5 million in the city to over 2 million in the city and surrounding suburbs. With a total population in Lebanon of approximately 6 million people, this means nearly one-third of the total Lebanese population lives in or around the capital city.

Beirut has been an important commercial center since over a thousand years before Christ, despite its temporary disappearance for over a century after it was destroyed by a fire in 140 BCE. It has been rebuilt many times since, first by the Romans under Pompey and most recently in the 1990s after the civil war. It was first conquered by the Arabs in 635 CE, and it became a significant center of commerce under the Ottomans. The life story of the city mirrors Lebanon's history.

Beirut is a major seaport and handles the bulk of the country's imports and exports. The city has important rail, road, and air connections to other parts of the country as well as to other cities in the Middle East and Europe.

TRIPOLI Known in Arabic as Tarabolous, Tripoli is Lebanon's second-largest city after it's capital and the largest city in the northern part of the country. Like Beirut, Tripoli is an ancient city that housed one of the most important ports in the world. Today, the city's port district, located 2 miles (3 km) from the city center on a small peninsula, continues to contribute to the country's economic well being.

The city of Tripoli has an ancient heritage. Founded in 700 BCE by the Phoenicians, it was taken by Muslims in 638 CE and held by them until 1109, when the Crusaders conquered and occupied the city. It has a famous old Frankish castle, Saint Gilles, which many tourists visit. In 1289, the Egyptians destroyed the city, but it was later rebuilt. It became an important city under the Ottomans.

Today, Tripoli's major industries include olive harvesting and processing, soap manufacturing, tobacco cultivation, sugar refining, and sponge fishing.

SIDON The third-largest city in Lebanon, Sidon, also has an illustrious history and boasts a castle dating back to the Crusades. Known as Sayda, or "fishery," in Arabic, this city lies 25 miles (40 km) to the south of Beirut. Sidon used to be a small fishing village, although it has grown in importance over the past hundred years. The city dates its heritage back much further than that, however. It was named after a grandson of the biblical Noah, and Jesus Christ preached a sermon along the coast of Sidon to his followers.

Sidon is situated in the southwest of the country. It is commercially important as a center for the export of olive oil and fruit. Known as the "city of gardens" since Persian times, Sidon today is still surrounded by citrus and banana plantations. Tobacco and figs, too, are cultivated in the surrounding countryside.

A twelfth-century
Frankish castle
foregrounds the
city of Sidon.

TYRE Another ancient city with biblical importance is Tyre, known as Soûr, or "rock," in Arabic. Tyre gets its name from the rocks upon which the city was originally built nearly five thousand years ago. It quickly became an economic hothouse from which Tyrian merchants set sail to sell their wares and discover new parts of the Mediterranean. It is said that Tyre provided the eighty thousand craftsmen who built King Solomon's palace in the tenth century BCE. Tyre's history might date back even further; the famous ancient Greek historian Herodotus stated that the city was built in the twenty-eighth century BCE, and that Zeus himself fell in love with a daughter of a Tyrian merchant.

Tyre was the most important city in ancient Phoenicia. The Phoenicians extracted a highly valued dye from a shellfish, which became known as Tyrian purple. Cloth of this color was available only in this area at the time. Like Tripoli, Tyre was captured by Muslims in the seventh century CE. In the twelfth century, it was taken over by the Crusaders, who held it until 1291, when Muslim rule was reestablished. In 1982, as a result of a war between the Arabs and Israel, Tyre was badly damaged. With much of its central area surrounded by squatter settlements, Tyre today is still being rebuilt.

BYBLOS Byblos, also known as Jubayl, is a small town—not even a city— located 22 miles (36 km) north of Beirut. Byblos is not known for its size or its grandeur but for being possibly the oldest continually inhabited city in the

world. Archaeological excavations have revealed that the site was first settled around 8800 BCE. Ancient philosophers even stated that the city was founded by Kronos, the father of Zeus and one of the oldest Greek gods in the pantheon. Archaeologists today state that Byblos has been continually inhabited since at least 5000 BCE, and there is evidence of trade between the ancient Egyptians in 2800 BCE and inhabitants of Byblos. This, in fact, is how Byblos received its name: Egyptians arrived in Byblos to barter for the papyrus they used as paper to write upon. The Greek word for book—*biblos*—comes from this ancient heritage.

Byblos is also the site of the first Crusader castle built in the Levant, a name given to the countries along the eastern shores of the Mediterranean Sea.

OTHER CITIES While most cities in Lebanon have historical importance, many of them also have become economically important—at least in the modern world—in recent years. These cities include Jounieh, which was once a small village and now is the fourth-largest city in the country. Today, it is known for its sunny resorts along the Mediterranean and its active nightlife. Aley is another city that became well known relatively late in its history. Located less than 10 miles (16 km) north of Beirut on the road to Damascus, Syria, this town became an important tourist destination for wealthy Lebanese and Arabs following the construction of the Beirut-Damascus Railway in the late nineteenth century. Today, it is a bustling resort city, known as the "Bride of the Summer." It is also notable for its high-altitude location, foggy days, and for having the largest Druze population in the world.

SPONGE FISHING

The sponges that occupied a place at most kitchen sinks before the invention of plastic sponges were the skeletons of a marine species found throughout the world. And if your kitchen or bath had one of the best quality sponges, it is possible the skeleton belonged to a marine animal scooped out of the Mediterranean Sea by a Lebanese fisherman.

Sponges are multicellular animals whose surface layer of cells covers an inner layer of flagellated cells (flagella are whiplike appendages) that move water through the animal, collecting food and providing a form of propulsion. There are numerous varieties of sponges throughout the world, but those found in the Mediterranean Sea are rated the best because of the softness of their skeletons.

Sponges are collected by fishermen who dive into the sea for them. The animal tissue is left in the sun to decompose; then the skeletal tissue, which does not decompose, is washed and bleached. Large sponges are cut into the familiar blocks that eventually find their way onto the shelves of specialty stores.

INTERNET LINKS

http://www.skileb.com/ski-lebanon/climate
Ski Lebanon provides information about Lebanon's climate and mountains, written for ski enthusiasts.

http://www.worldatlas.com/webimage/countrys/asia/lebanon/lbland.htm
This World Atlas website gives many facts about Lebanon's geography, along with detailed maps.

Sidon was inhabited as early as 4000 BCE. For the ancients, it was such an important city that it was praised by the Greek writer Homer, who commented on the skill of Sidonian glassworkers.

HISTORY

2

WHILE THE LEBANESE LIVED IN relative peace for many years under Ottoman rule, the twentieth and twenty-first centuries have not been kind to them. The country has experienced much instability and war since the end of World War II, including its own civil war from 1975 to 1990. Following the civil war, Lebanon had to rebuild itself. Since then, the country has often delved back into chaos due to religious or political strife, often involving its neighbors Syria and Israel. It is indeed tragic that a country like Lebanon, with such an illustrious heritage and such importance in the development of human civilization, has experienced so many years of war and devastation.

The Phoenician alphabet is the oldest confirmed alphabet in the world. Developed around 1200 BCE, the alphabet consists of twenty-two consonants. Spread through Phoenician trade, it became one of the most widely used ancient alphabets in the world.

EARLY INHABITANTS

While little is known of the first inhabitants of Lebanon, archaeologists have uncovered proof that settlements date back to at least 5000 BCE.

These prehistoric people lived in small communities along the coast, where they could survive on fishing and growing crops in the rich alluvial soil.

Similar land is also found in the Bekáa Valley, and there, too, early farmers settled down after migrating from Mesopotamia, home of the very early Sumerian and Babylonian civilizations. The excavation of a kiln-fired clay sculpture dating back to 3000 BCE is evidence of this. It is a figure of Astarte, also known as Ishtar, who was originally a Mesopotamian mother goddess of love and war. Other terra-cotta figures from around this period have also been found—nearly all are of nude female figures.

Finds of terra-cotta figures bearing elaborate hairstyles and jewelry show the influence of ancient Egyptian culture in the Levant. Pharaoh Ramses II (ca. 1304—1213 BCE) passed through Lebanon in his war against the Hittites, whom he defeated in what is now Syria. The Obelisk Temple at Byblos clearly shows an Egyptian influence in its style and design.

Also in the ancient town of Byblos, excavations have exposed town walls that date back to the Amorite period. "Amorite" is a general term for early groups of Semitic people who established communities in the Levant in

Old Testament times. Amorite settlements along the coast were, naturally, engaged in local maritime trade and would also have traded with inland communities in what is now Syria and Jordan. Out of such a background there developed the first known commercial empire on Earth, Phoenicia.

THE PHOENICIANS

Phoenicia, established in approximately 1500 BCE along the coast of the Mediterranean Sea, would eventually become a powerful empire under which various city-states operated. The word "Phoenicia" itself likely comes from the Greek word for purple, which refers to the purple dye produced and made famous by Tyre. That city would become the Phoenician capital in 1000 BCE during the high point of Phoenician civilization. From there, Phoenicians launched boats to explore the world, mainly through trading. They also established other city-states, including Carthage, in modern-day Tunisia, in the ninth century BCE.

Phoenician Merchant Ship Arriving in Pharos by Albert Sebille

DISCOVERERS OF AMERICA?

It is possible that the Phoenicians discovered America some two thousand years before either the Vikings in the tenth century CE or the expedition five hundred years later led by Christopher Columbus. The evidence for putting forward this theory is partly based on the known seafaring prowess of the Phoenicians. They are believed to have sailed down the west coast of Africa and, in other expeditions, probably reached the southwest of Britain.

Research has also revealed similarities between pre-Columbian American and Mediterranean civilizations. There are parallel examples in metallurgy, agriculture, mathematics, and language between Phoenician culture and those of the Olmecs and Mayas of the Americas.

One example given to support the claim of a cultural link is a dwarflike god, Bes, whose image adorned the prows of Phoenician ships. A "twin" dwarflike god has also been found in statues of the Olmec culture in Central America and of the Mayas of South America. What gives some weight to this example is that the American god is always shown with a beard, while in pre-Columbian American culture men did not grow beards. The bearded dwarf, it is claimed, crossed the Atlantic with his Phoenician admirers.

The reason why the Phoenicians were able to establish their empire across the Mediterranean was because trading brought them immense profits. The Phoenicians traded linen, metal, glass, wood, ivory, precious stones, and wine. They would obtain goods from areas to which they had traveled—such as silver from Sardinia—and then trade it at commercial outposts along the Mediterranean coast. However, sometime around the sixth century BCE,

Phoenicia began its decline. It was first conquered by the Persians, led by Cyrus the Great, and then by the Macedonian king Alexander the Great. Eventually, it would become part of the Roman Empire, during which time Lebanon was Christianized.

THE ROMAN EMPIRE

The Roman general Pompey the Great conquered Phoenicia in 64 BCE, incorporating it into the Roman Empire. But Pompey did not end there. Using Phoenicia, and more specifically modern-day Lebanon, as a military base, he led successful wars against Armenia and Syria. With Lebanon as a launching base, the Roman Empire captured most of the territory in the Levant, including the city of Jerusalem.

The Romans wanted top-quality timber for their ships and buildings, and they found just what they needed in the forests of modern-day Lebanon. They kept guard over the forests and built roads to transport logs to the coast,

When the Roman general Pompey the Great conquered Phoenicia, Lebanon became part of the Roman Empire.

from where they could be shipped to Rome. The Romans are famous for the roads they built and carefully maintained. Roman milestones, recording the completion of road repairs, have been found in Lebanon.

MUSLIM CONQUEST

In 630 CE, Muslim Arabs conquered the territory of Syria, of which modern-day Lebanon was a part. This occurred during the first expansion of Islam outside of the Arabian Peninsula, shortly after the Prophet Muhammad's death, when caliphs, or religious successors to Muhammad, expanded both their religious and political power. Known as the Umayyads (oo-MY-ahdz), they ruled until 750, when they were conquered by new caliphs, the Abbasids (ah-BAH-sidz). The Abbasids moved their capital from Damascus in Syria to Baghdad in modern-day Iraq.

Under the caliphate, Christians were allowed to practice their religion, but they were discriminated against and lost social and political power. In 759 and again in 760, there were revolts by Christian communities, but those rebellions were easily repressed.

As a result of the violent struggle between the Umayyads and the Abbasids, local dynasties emerged in Lebanon. A more centralized Muslim rule, however, was established again after the rise of the Mamluks, also known as Mamelukes, who overthrew the Abbasids in 1250.

CHRISTIAN CRUSADERS

Even before Christian Crusaders arrived in Lebanon during the holy wars in the late eleventh century, the area around Mount Lebanon was known as a refuge for persecuted minorities. Christian Maronites, who followed the fourth-century Christian saint Maron, had settled there since the seventh century. Muslim Druze, who were viewed as heretics by the larger Muslim community, had fled to the southern Lebanon Mountains soon after their religion's establishment in the eleventh century.

The majority of the Crusaders came from France, Germany, and Italy, with some from England. The Arabs called all of them Franks. The first

Although there are several traditional sites for the tomb of the biblical figure Noah, residents of the town of Karak in the Bekáa Valley have long claimed that the true tomb of the patriarch is within their village.

The tomb has been documented since at least the tenth century and can still be seen today. It is over 100 feet (20 m) long, and its size is often attributed to the fact that it was constructed from an ancient Roman aqueduct. A Roman inscription in Latin, dated to the first century CE, pays homage to the man in the tomb, referring to him as the "man with many names."

Crusade expedition arrived in 1099 and the last one remained until the fourteenth century. The aim of the Crusades was to secure Christian rule over the Muslim-controlled holy places of the eastern Mediterranean, as Christian communities had been finding it increasingly difficult to withstand the growing influence of Islam in the country.

THE OTTOMAN EMPIRE

The Mamluk Muslim dynasties lasted from 1250 until the Ottoman sultan Selim I conquered them in the early sixteenth century. The Ottomans had just conquered the Persians and would continue to take over large swaths of territory in the eastern Mediterranean. This began the Ottoman Empire, which was based more on economic control than religious ideology. This meant that non-Muslim and different Muslim sects were allowed to practice their religions in peace, as long as they paid their taxes and were loyal to Ottoman rule.

The more powerful local families were put in charge of collecting the taxes, and they became the base for influential dynasties that began to emerge in the late sixteenth and early seventeenth centuries. Descendants of some of these powerful families still dominate Lebanese politics. Two main dynasties controlled the political scene: the Maans and, later, the Shihabs. They formed alliances with various Muslim and Christian groups, chiefly the Druze and Maronites, but switching allegiances among the different power groups led to an instability in Lebanese politics that boded ill for the future.

Constant rivalry between Muslim and Christian groups took the form of religious conflicts, but they often disguised deeper economic inequalities among different groups of people. Increasing animosity between landlords and peasants, and political differences between Druze and Maronite groups came to a head in 1858, and a fierce civil war raged for two years. It ended with an apparent victory for the Druze, but in 1859, foreign troops from European powers and the Ottoman Empire arrived in the country and established a new administration. This ensured that a Christian ruler governed the country,

World War I soldiers visit Baalbek in Lebanon.

although Lebanon remained part of the Ottoman Empire. This arrangement lasted until World War I (1914—1918).

The world was plunged into war in the early twentieth century, and countries were divided based on loyalties to their allies. After the war, as during the war, this would cause grave consequences when the victors took over the spoils of those who had lost. The Ottoman Empire supported Germany during World War I, and when they lost, the three main Allied powers (Britain, France, and Russia) divided the territories that had belonged to the vanquished. This meant that Lebanon was no longer part of the Ottoman Empire, which was dismantled. Instead, it became a territory of the French.

The French created the modern borders of Lebanon and established its identity as a separate country. Before that, the territory had always been part of larger provinces governed by empires based in Rome, Damascus, Medina, and Constantinople. The French brought together the Muslim coastal areas and the inland Christian mountain area into one administrative region.

Many Muslims were reluctant to accept their new identity as Lebanese because they saw the new country as being Western and Christian. The French and the Maronites supported one another, and when the new Lebanese government was organized in 1926, the Christians were left in a politically powerful position. The French had created one country but not a unified people. The basic conflict between Christian groups who looked to the West and Muslim groups who looked to the Arab world was an underlying cause of a civil war that would return Lebanon to the fractured conditions that existed before the French took over.

THE FRENCH MANDATE AND INDEPENDENCE

In 1926, the Lebanese Republic was created with the establishment of a new constitution, which was written to maintain equality in government between different religious groups. However, Lebanon was still under French control. World War II (1939—1945) provided the opportunity for the country's parliament to declare its independence, which it did in 1943 when France was occupied by Germany. Unhappy with losing their territory, the French promptly threw the recently elected Lebanese president and prime minister in jail. The Lebanese responded with a general uprising and, combined with international pressure, France backed down and released the prisoners.

As has often happened in history, the colonial power in Lebanon left behind a state of instability and conflict that it had largely created. A power-sharing system was set up in which government posts were divided between representatives of the main religious groups. A compromise was reached: the Christians renounced allegiance to the West, and the Muslims renounced union with Syria or other Arab states. The effect, however, was to institutionalize the differences between the religious groups, and because the Christians were given a disproportionate share of power, a bitter resentment arose among the increasing number of poor Shiite Muslims, also called Shia Muslims.

The powerful Christian lobby, meanwhile, began to express a wish to ally itself with the West and distance itself from the neighboring Arab world. Muslims naturally wished to have closer cooperation with other Arab states, and there were two coups, in 1949 and 1961, aimed at forming a union with Syria. In 1958, the first outbreak of war in Lebanon occurred when Lebanese people responded to the Pan-Arab call of Egyptian president Gamal

The state of Greater Lebanon was proclaimed on September 1, 1920.

A massacre that killed up to 3,500 Palestinian refugees during the Lebanese civil war occurred in September 1982. As retaliation for the assassination of newly elected Christian president Bachir Gemayel, Christian militias entered the adjacent Sabra and Shatila camps in Beirut on September 16. There they carried out a massacre against any Palestinian refugee in their path—men, women, and children. This attack lasted until September 18 and was observed, without interference, by the Christian militias' Israeli allies.

In December 1982, the United Nations General Assembly unanimously condemned the Sabra and Shatila massacre and classified it as an act of genocide. It remains one of the most horrific episodes of the Lebanese civil war.

Abdel Nasser. The United States intervened for the first time in response to President Camille Chamoun's request for assistance against internal opposition and threats. By rendering support to the government, the United States successfully displaced opposing forces. The aftermath of the operation saw General Fuad Chehab replacing Camille Chamoun as president.

In 1970, the Palestine Liberation Organization (PLO) moved its headquarters to Lebanon after being expelled from Jordan. As the Arab-Israeli conflict deepened, Palestinians expelled from Israel sought refuge in Lebanon, where other Palestinians had fled when the state of Israel was created in 1948. By 1975, Palestinians in Lebanon numbered more than three hundred thousand. Raids across the border into the Jewish state added to the tensions that were beginning to tear Lebanon apart.

CIVIL WAR

The civil war began in 1975 as tensions continued to escalate between Christian and Muslim factions, spurred on by the increase in Muslim Palestinian refugees in the country and general Christian fears that they would lose representation in government. It officially began when shots were fired into a church congregation where the Christian president was worshipping.

In 1983, terrorist bombs killed more than three hundred American and French troops, and Western forces eventually pulled out of Lebanon. This allowed civil conflict to erupt once more. Westerners in Beirut became the target of Muslim kidnappers in 1984, and in 1987, Syrian troops occupied Beirut. In the south of the country, the Israeli army continued to battle with Palestinian troops. Beirut became a city divided: East Beirut was Christian; West Beirut was Muslim. The demarcation line between the two became known as the Green Line, and this border was often the scene of fierce fighting. The country was governed by a bewildering array of militias, each of which controlled its own territory. Over the next two years, Lebanon teetered on the brink of collapse. The rival Muslim and Christian groups could not agree on who should be president.

THE TAIF AGREEMENT

In 1989, a committee formed by the Arab League gathered in Taif, Saudi Arabia, to work on political solutions to ending the long civil war in Lebanon.

The fruit of their labor was the Taif Agreement, also known as the National Reconciliation Accord, which set about the terms that would end the war. The document gave increased power to Muslims in Lebanon and set a timeline for Syrian withdrawal from the country. It was signed on October 22, 1989, and ratified by the Lebanese parliament several weeks later. Slightly over a year later, Western hostages held in Lebanon were released, and the Green Line dividing Beirut was dismantled. The war was finally over.

In 1992, voting for a new National Assembly took place for the first time in twenty years—seventeen years after the first incidents that had led to the civil war. The elected prime minister, Rafiq al-Hariri, set about rebuilding war-ravaged Beirut.

The end of the civil war found most militias weakened or disbanded. Palestinian troops that used to occupy southern Lebanon as a base for attacking Israel withdrew in May 2000. The assassination of Rafiq al-Hariri in 2005 triggered the Cedar Revolution, in which Lebanese groups demanded that Syria withdraw its fifteen-thousand-strong army forces as well as end its interference in Lebanese affairs. In April 2005, Syria finally withdrew from Lebanon. Since then, there have been increased periods of tension and political instability, particularly between 2006 and 2008, when conflicts with the Shia militia group in Lebanon, Hezbollah, led to war.

INTERNET LINKS

http://almashriq.hiof.no/lebanon/900/902/Kamal-Salibi
Read excerpts from *A House of Many Mansions: The History of Lebanon Reconsidered* by Kamal Salibi.

http://www.bbc.com/news/world-middle-east-14649284
This BBC timeline records important events in Lebanon's history.

GOVERNMENT

Members of parliament discuss as they cast votes for the Lebanese president in 2014.

3

FOLLOWING ITS FIFTEEN-YEAR CIVIL war, Lebanon's government had the enormous task of rebuilding itself to reflect the new needs of its people. Given the demographic change that had, in part, catalyzed the civil war, Muslims were given more representation in their government than before.

Before 1943, political control of the country had only been in the hands of the president, who, according to the constitution, must be a Maronite Christian. Following Lebanese independence, however, political authority was divided between the Christian president and the Muslim prime minister. Furthermore, there was a more equitable divide between religious groups in the 128-member parliament. However, these stipulations, while warranted and helpful, have also led to challenges in recent years. Lebanon was without a president from 2014 until former prime minister Michel Aoun's appointment in 2016, in part due to a lack of consensus among different groups in the Lebanese parliament.

POLITICAL SYSTEM

The Lebanese constitution was drafted in 1926, before the country even declared independence from France. Since then, the constitution has been amended multiple times, most notably in 1989 with the Taif Agreement. The constitution sets forth Lebanon as a republic with universal suffrage, meaning every adult citizen age twenty-one and over

In October 2016, in a surprise move, former Lebanese prime minister Saad al-Hariri voiced his support for his political enemy, Michel Aoun, to become president, stating that there was no other choice to resolve the country's political deadlock. Aoun, a Christian who has allied with Hezbollah, was elected to office on October 31, 2016, to wide support.

The signing of the Taif Agreement in 1989 brought an end to Lebanon's bloody civil war.

has the right to vote. It also mandates the distribution of government offices based on confessionalism, or on the proportional distribution of governmental power based on religious communities.

The formal head of government is the prime minister, who is chosen by the president in consultation with the 128 members of the National Assembly. Elections to the National Assembly normally take place every four years. The last election was held in 2009. The National Assembly at that time was made up of the Rafiq Hariri Martyr List with seventy-one seats, the Amal-Hezbollah alliance with thirty seats, and the Free Patriotic Movement with twenty-seven seats. By custom, the president is a Maronite Christian, the prime minister is a Sunni Muslim, and the speaker of the National Assembly is a Shiite Muslim. This tripartite division based on religion dates back to 1943 when the country first achieved independence. At that time an agreement was made that all government bodies would be proportioned on the basis of six Christians to five Muslims. This division was always unfair because Christians did not make up a majority of the population. It gave undue power to the Christians and caused resentment and conflict. This eventually led to the civil war that ended with a new constitution, formalized in 1990 following the Taif Agreement, giving Muslims their proper majority voice in the running of the country. From 2014 until 2016, the parliament was unable to reach the quorum necessary to appoint the Christian president. Finally, on October 31, 2016, political and religious groups in parliament were able to agree on the election of former prime minister Michel Aoun.

HEZBOLLAH

Hezbollah (also known as Hizbollah) is a radical Shiite Muslim organization. It developed among poor residents of southern Lebanon in response to Israel's occupation of their land in 1982, and was subsequently funded by

Iran. Hezbollah means "Party of God" in Arabic, and they follow a militant political and religious ideology. Hezbollah has grown more powerful in recent years, which is often ascribed to the large amounts of funding it continues to receive from Iran.

Hezbollah is engaged in both peaceful politics and armed conflicts. It has representatives in the Lebanese parliament. Its funding from Iran allows it to develop and maintain an extensive social welfare program for the poorest sections of Lebanese society. Much-needed hospitals, schools, and food stores are run by Hezbollah, and it gives assistance that the central government is not yet able to provide. Hezbollah also has an influential TV station called al-Manar (The Lighthouse).

Hezbollah demonstrators march through the streets of Ourai, Lebanon.

After Israel's withdrawal from south Lebanon in 2000 and the retreat of Syrian troops in 2005, Hezbollah became the most powerful military force in Lebanon. It is currently under pressure to demilitarize and integrate its forces into the Lebanese army. Hezbollah is classified by some countries, including the United States, as a terrorist organization. Other countries, including the United Kingdom, have declared that solely Hezbollah's military branch can be classified as a terrorist organization.

REGIONAL TENSIONS

Lebanon has had past border disputes with both of its neighbors: Syria and Israel. As of 2008, diplomatic relations between Syria and Lebanon have been reinstated. However, Syria's long and devastating civil war has occasionally spilled over into Lebanon.

As for Israel, tensions remain between the two countries. Israel occupied 19 square miles (49 sq km) of heavily contested land—referred to as Shebaa Farms on the northwestern slope of Mount Hermon, at the junction of Lebanon, Syria, and Israel—from 2000 until 2006. While Israel still continues to control the area, fighting ended with the 2006 Lebanon War. However, this

MR. MIRACLE

Rafiq al-Hariri, who became Lebanon's prime minister after the end of the civil war and held the post until his resignation in 2004, was nicknamed Mr. Miracle by Lebanese newspapers. He was an extremely rich man and was recognized as one of the world's hundred wealthiest people. As prime minister, he had set himself the task of spearheading the rebuilding of his country and played an important role in jumpstarting Lebanon's international investment and economic revival. He put $100 million into an investment project for the rebuilding of Beirut, and, since 1982, he paid university fees for thirty thousand Lebanese studying at home and abroad.

It has been said that he would indeed have to be a Mr. Miracle to survive as Lebanon's leading politician. Many political leaders have been assassinated by rival groups, and Rafiq al-Hariri required massive security to thwart the attempts on his life. He personally employed forty private bodyguards and drove in a convoy of six armored Mercedes accompanied by armed soldiers in other vehicles. The central government offices were equipped with blast-resistant armor plating and bulletproof glass. In spite of these precautions, al-Hariri was assassinated on February 14, 2005, by explosives when his convoy was in Beirut. His assassination remains under investigation, although Hezbollah operatives were indicted through the International Court of Justice in 2011. In June 2005, the Beirut International Airport was renamed Beirut Rafiq Hariri International Airport in his honor.

does not mean that fighting cannot reignite at some point. Tensions between Lebanon and Israel—particularly over land control and Israel's position in the Middle East—continue.

The Shebaa Farms conflict was largely responsible for cross-border attacks throughout 2006, including the thirty-four-day Lebanon War. Fought between Hezbollah and Israel, this was the first time since Israel's War of Independence in 1948 that rockets had landed in major cities like Haifa and killed several dozen Israelis.

The Lebabon War began on July 12, 2006, when Hezbollah fired multiple rockets at Israeli military bases and border villages. This was actually a diversionary tactic that was staged to capture two Israeli soldiers as hostages for the exchange of Arab prisoners in Israeli jails. Israel retaliated with air strikes and artillery attacks, and by imposing an air and naval blockade, as well as launching a major ground invasion of southern Lebanon. In the wake of the Israeli attacks, some 130,000 homes, 350 schools, and 2 hospitals were destroyed. Numerous sewage plants and 400 miles (644 km) of road were also damaged. It was estimated that the damage done to Lebanese infrastructure amounts to a staggering $7 billion to $10 billion. About a month later, the United Nations passed a resolution to end the conflict, calling for Israel's withdrawal, the disarming of Hezbollah, and the deployment of Lebanese soldiers in southern Lebanon. Both Israel and Lebanon agreed to the cessation of retaliatory attacks. As part of the UN proposal, the number of United Nations Interim Forces in Lebanon (UNIFIL) was increased in southern Lebanon to restore and maintain the peace.

The massacre at the Sabra and Shatila Palestinian refugee camps in 1982 was one of the bloodiest moments of the Lebanese civil war.

In 2016, analysts warned that another war could be the horizon between Hezbollah and Israel, due to Hezbollah setting up bases in contested border areas in an attempt to support the Syrian regime in its civil war. Since the beginning of the Syrian civil war, Hezbollah has acquired more weapons, including rockets, mortars, and tanks, in cross-border fighting. Increased tensions in the area could cause a far more devastating war to break out between Hezbollah and Israel than the war in 2006.

CIVIL RIGHTS

In a country that has been in a near constant state of war for the past thirty years, it should come as no surprise that human rights have suffered.

THE LEBANESE ARMED FORCES

Some of the Lebanese Armed Forces' (LAF) primary missions are maintaining security and stability in the country, guarding the country's borders and ports, relief and rescue operations, firefighting, and combating drug trafficking. The army, air force, and navy make up the three branches of the LAF, and they are operated and coordinated by the LAF Command in Yarzeh, east of Beirut. Lebanon has six military colleges and schools. Promising cadets may be sent to other countries to receive further training.

Beside the commando and artillery regiments, the Lebanese army is also made up of the Republican Guard Brigade, which is responsible for protecting the president by traveling with him.

The air force currently lacks operational capability. The few fighter pilot aircraft it owns are old and of no use in combat. However, Lebanon does invest in active aircraft like helicopters that are used on a variety of domestic missions, mainly in battling narcotics trafficking and other violations.

The Lebanese navy, on the other hand, is very active. It is charged with protecting Lebanon's waters and ports and for keeping watch over illegal smuggling of goods.

Previously, Lebanon had mandatory military service of one year for men. In May 2005, the new conscription system reduced compulsory service to only a six-month period. Mandatory military service was completely phased out as of February 10, 2007.

The 2006 Lebanon War killed over 1,500 Lebanese civilians and displaced about 1 million others.

According to many, human rights are now on par with global standards, yet civil rights activists have still pointed out long periods of detention and even torture among security forces. Palestinians have fewer civil rights than other groups in the country. They are not allowed to own houses or land, and are being restricted from certain professions.

There are a number of different courts in Lebanon. Besides the regular civilian court, there is also a military court that handles all cases involving members of military groups. There are also religious tribunals for the various Muslim and Christian denominations. These handle disputes involving marriage and inheritance. Every citizen is entitled to a lawyer unless he or she can't afford to pay for one, which means that poor people are at a serious disadvantage in the courtroom.

THE PRESIDENT

The president of the republic is elected by parliament to serve a nonrenewable six-year term. The president of Lebanon from 2008 to 2014 was Michel Suleiman. Prior to becoming president, Suleiman was commander in chief of the Lebanese Armed Forces. When Suleiman's term came to an end in 2014, no candidate received the two-thirds majority vote required by law in the National Assembly to take his place for two years.

In 2016, political divisions were repaired when different political parties and religious groups announced that they would support Michel Aoun for president. Aoun is a former Lebanese army commander and the founder of the Free Patriotic Movement, a majority Christian party that has formed an alliance with Hezbollah. Aoun played a large role in the civil war and even acted as contested prime minister for several months before the end of the war, before fleeing to France in fear for his life. Michel Aoun was elected as president of Lebanon on October 31, 2016.

In the refugee camps, Palestinian groups operate their courts, and Hezbollah and the Islamic militia conduct theirs in a similar manner. In the cases heard in the camps, Islamic law is applied to them, causing occasional conflicts with the laws of Lebanon.

INTERNET LINKS

http://www.lebanonembassyus.org/lebanese-government.html
The Embassy of Lebanon in the United States provides great information on its website about the Lebanese government and various ministries.

http://www.loc.gov/law/help/lebanon-constitutional-law.php
This in-depth report provides a summary of the Taif Agreement and the National Pact.

Political assassinations have continued in Lebanon since the death of Rafiq al-Hariri in 2005. Since November 2006 and as recently as 2013, many prominent figures, including Lebanese cabinet minister Pierre Gemayel, top security advisor Wissam al-Hassan, and former finance minister Mohamad Chatah, have been killed.

ECONOMY

The Lebanese pound, or the livre, is the national currency of Lebanon.

4

SINCE THE END OF ITS LONG CIVIL war, Lebanon has attempted to improve its economy—and with some success. Lebanon's gross domestic product (GDP) grew about 9 percent in 2010 despite a global economic slump. However, the Syrian civil war has put a damper on Lebanon's finances in recent years. While its economy is still labeled as stable, Lebanon's GDP growth shrank starting in 2011 to 2 percent or less each year, and the country's debt-to-GDP ratio remains one of the highest in the world.

According to the World Bank, public spending in Lebanon increased by $1 billion from 2012 to 2014 due to the Syrian civil war and the influx of Syrian refugees into the country. Overall losses due to the war during this period are calculated at $7.5 billion.

BEFORE THE CIVIL WAR

Before Lebanon's civil war began in 1975, the country was economically stable and ranked as one of the top thirty-five upper-middle-income countries of the world. The three main financial sectors were trade, banking, and tourism. In particular, the tourist industry was strong in Lebanon, with tourists flocking there from all over the world to enjoy the country's beautiful climate and historic sites. However, during the instability of the war, the tourism industry was destroyed. Tourism

A Beirut marketplace in 1969

relies on stability and safety, and it is not surprising that tourists stopped visiting the country during this time.

Another problem was caused by the loss of central government control. A number of regions were controlled by local militias. The central government was unable to collect taxes in those areas, so the years of factional fighting seriously damaged Lebanon's economy. This resulted in rising unemployment and a very high rate of inflation, serious problems for those who are poor to begin with. As a result, the poor got poorer and the rich got richer.

AFTER THE CIVIL WAR

In the years since the civil war, Lebanon's economic outlook was seeming positive, despite its mounting debts. From 1992 to 1998, annual inflation fell more than 100 percent to 5 percent, and foreign exchange reserves also saw improvements in a rise to more than $6 billion from a previous $1.4 billion. Two of the factors for Lebanon's economic recovery were a sound banking system and international aid.

During this time, Lebanon developed a plan to rebuild its country, economically and otherwise, following the devastation of the war. This plan was called Horizon 2000. It was first announced in 1993, about eighteen months after the last shell of the civil war destroyed yet one more building in old Beirut. The goal was to restore Beirut to its pre-1975 status as a major international business and banking center. The total cost of Horizon 2000 was initially estimated at $13 billion, but spiraling costs made the final figure $20 billion.

By the end of the civil war, the country's infrastructure was in a state of serious disrepair. Only one in three of the country's telephones were working, and electricity was restricted to six hours a day in Beirut. Outside the capital, electricity was nonexistent in many places. Water was also in short supply, and when it was available, it was often polluted.

Lebanon is presently making only about $4.9 billion a year, while its total expenditure is at approximately $6.6 billion. Therefore, it is not surprising that Lebanon's public debt is an estimated 163 percent of its GDP. This means that aid is now required from international donors for loans at lower-than-usual interest rates.

The plan to rebuild the city center of Beirut was a controversial one, primarily because of the cost. The city's central area was previously the zone that bridged the east and west sides of the divided city during the civil war. So many buildings had been damaged that well over half of the area had to be demolished and cleared away before rebuilding could begin.

Although Beirut is now largely reconstructed, the huge debt that the Lebanese government accumulated had negative implications for its national economy and the Lebanese people. Critics say this unnecessary zeal to redo Beirut has led to neglect of the need to restore decent living conditions for ordinary citizens in other parts of the country. However, the plan worked. By 2006, bank assets in Lebanon reached $75 billion US. The war of 2006 again damaged Lebanon's economy—particularly impacting its tourism and banking industries—but it quickly recovered. Lebanese banks regained stability after the war, and the country's economy remained untouched by the global economic crisis in 2008. In fact, Lebanon was among the only countries in the world with an overall increase in its stock market in 2008. This changed in 2011 with the outbreak of the Syrian civil war. Very quickly, the war in Lebanon's neighboring country destabilized Lebanon itself, both socially and economically.

Beirut needed to be rebuilt following Lebanon's deadly—and costly—civil war.

THE SYRIAN CIVIL WAR

In March 2011, protests in Syria against its leader, Bashar al-Assad, turned into a full-blown civil war, pitting rebels against government loyalists.

The civil war in Syria has added increasing economic pressures to the Lebanese government.

Many Syrians fled the violence—and continue to flee the violence—by escaping to surrounding countries and/or eventually trying to flee to Europe. Lebanon has borne the brunt of Syrian refugee resettlement. From 2011 to 2016, it is estimated that 1.5 million Syrian refugees took refuge in Lebanon. This number becomes even more staggering when considering the total population of Lebanon before the influx of refugees was approximately 4.5 million.

While Lebanon's generosity to refugees is certainly laudable, it has had dire consequences for its economy. Public finances have been strained almost to the breaking point, and environmental resources have been tapped for refugee camps. Some estimates state that, since the war, two hundred thousand Lebanese nationals have fallen into poverty, with another three hundred thousand young Lebanese nationals unemployed. This has been caused by several factors related to the war, including a decrease in tourism in the area and increases in sectarian violence. In addition, Lebanon's proximity has posed security issues for the country, and ground transportation into Lebanon has almost entirely stopped, also ceasing many imports and exports.

As of September 2016, the International Monetary Fund (IMF) projected a 2.5 percent increase in economic activity over the next year. This was downgraded to 2 percent just one month later, in October. However, many Lebanese economists have stated that they believe this is still an overly optimistic number, and that Lebanon's economy will, in fact, be unstable or in decline over the coming years if the Syrian war is not resolved.

Indeed, Lebanon has experienced many years of war—both in the country and around its borders—but it has somehow always managed to stay afloat economically. The country may be challenged, however, with the duration and particular violence of the Syrian civil war.

NATURAL RESOURCES

While Lebanon does not have many mineral resources, its arable land is its greatest natural resource. The rich alluvial soil found in the country is excellent for cultivation and has bolstered the agricultural sector of the economy. Another important natural resource is limestone, which is quarried along Mount Lebanon. Iron ore and salt are also quarried there.

Lebanon's arable land is its greatest resource.

The country's fast-flowing rivers, especially the Litani, are being developed for hydroelectric power and for the irrigation of the surrounding agricultural land. So far there have been three hydroelectric plants built on the Litani, with the one in Bekáa Valley being Lebanon's largest power facility.

AGRICULTURE

Agriculture in Lebanon is responsible for approximately 5 percent of the country's GDP and employs 10 percent of the population. Outside of its major cities, Lebanon has a large amount of arable land, which is good for planting crops like wheat, barley, olives, grapes, and tobacco. In mountainous regions, terraces are cut into slopes that are covered in fertile soil.

Important farm products are grains, citrus fruit, figs, grapes, mulberries, apples, and bananas. Tomatoes, potatoes, and olives are also found on most farms. Between the years 2000 to 2005, agriculture contributed approximately 7.4 percent to Lebanon's GDP. This decreased to 5 percent in 2015, although it is still the country's fourth-largest employment sector.

The long, dry summer months cause a shortage of water for farmers who, over the centuries, have fine-tuned all available means of irrigation. One ambitious attempt to channel water to where it is most needed was the South Bekáa Irrigation Project, which harnessed the country's longest river, the Litani. As of 2008, this project had irrigated over 16,556 acres (6,700 ha) of land.

While once Lebanon was a major player in the production and distribution of narcotics, primarily opium and hashish, government regulation largely stopped the illicit drug trafficking trade—at least, until the Syrian civil war. At its peak in 1988, the sale of narcotics brought in a staggering $1.5 billion to Lebanon. However, in 2009, the Lebanese government cracked down on cannabis and opium production in the Bekáa Valley and destroyed almost all of those crops. The crackdown on illicit drug operations in Lebanon was previously halted due to increased conflicts between 2005 and 2007, before being reinstated in 2008.

However, drug trafficking between Lebanon and Syria has increased in recent years due to the lack of border control during the civil war. A recent report suggests that drugs such as amphetamines are now being manufactured in Lebanon to be brought to fighters in the Syrian war. The market for amphetamines is in high demand now among Syrian fighters who use these drugs to fuel their fighting.

Another ambitious endeavor is the Litani Water Project, which will cost $460 million to implement. Once completed, it will benefit ninety-nine villages and thousands of acres of agricultural land in the south. With loans from Kuwait and the Arab Development Fund, the first phase of the project is currently under way. The second phase will focus on a series of twenty-two irrigation networks that will provide water to 37,065 acres (15,000 ha) of land in the south.

INDUSTRY

Main industries in Lebanon are metal fabrication, banking, food processing, cement, textiles, mineral and chemical products, and wood and furniture products. Most industrial companies are family owned and are located in and around Beirut. The government has provided industrial companies with fiscal incentives, including tax exemptions and lower customs duties, in order to promote the growth of industry within Lebanon.

DEVELOPMENT

Lebanon was rapidly developed both in the years preceding the civil war and in the years following. In the chaos of rebuilding the country, and in particular Beirut, the construction boom led to a rapid increase in real estate prices. This also attracted foreign investment into Lebanon from Gulf Arab investors, who saw this construction as an attractive investment opportunity.

Textile production is an important industry in Lebanon.

Lebanon also hosts Project Lebanon, an international trade fair for construction technology, materials, and equipment. This yearly affair serves as a platform for potential investors from international companies to showcase their products and services and also to explore opportunities for themselves in the building and construction sector in Lebanon.

TRADE

Faced with a lack of natural resources and constrained by its size, Lebanon has always imported far more than it exports. Consumer goods make up most of the imports into Lebanon, as well as cars, livestock, clothing, medicinal products, machinery, and petroleum products.

Despite its trade imbalance, prior to the civil war Lebanon was not in danger of falling into increasing debt. It had been able to earn vast sums of money from what economists call invisible earnings. Tourists visiting the country spent their foreign currencies, and this was a major source of invisible earnings. Even more profitable was income earned through financial dealings involving banking and insurance.

The main exports are agricultural products, chemicals, precious and semiprecious metals, construction minerals, electric power machinery, paper, and jewelry. The principal countries that trade with Lebanon are neighboring

This jewelry worker in Beirut is putting the finishing touches on a gold ring. Jewelry such as this is one of Lebanon's main exports.

Middle East states, France, Germany, Switzerland, Italy, China, the United Kingdom, and the United States.

THE BANKING INDUSTRY

For most of the twentieth century, until the beginning of the Lebanese civil war, Beirut was the undisputed banking capital of the Middle East. Following the civil war, the leaders of the country agreed that reestablishing the banking industry was their main goal. This was a success, and within several years, Lebanon's banking sector again provided the foundation for their economy. One reason why Beirut has been so successful is because it has developed into a trusted international financial center due to its banking secrecy laws. Like Zurich and other renowned banking capitals, Beirut offers its investors high levels of security, privacy, and protection. Lebanese banks are also known for strictly adhering to international regulations and standards, as well as for successfully managing risk assessment. This combination of stringent regulation and investor trust meant that Lebanon's banks were some of the only banks in the world to weather the 2008 global financial crisis.

Despite conflicts in the region, Lebanese banks recorded a 5.5 percent annual growth in net profits in the first half of 2013. Lebanese banks have also expanded around the world and are entering markets across the Middle East, North Arica, and Australia. Lebanese banks are currently located in over thirty-one cities on five continents. By 2013, Lebanese banks increased customer deposits by 8.8 percent to $134.19 billion. Their total balance sheets increased by 7.83 percent to approximately $158.56 billion. Another sure sign that Beirut is recapturing international trust and recognition is the fact that familiar American fast-food chains have opened branches in the city.

Lebanon's natural beauty, mild climate, historic legacy, and strategic proximity to the Mediterranean Sea have made it a popular choice for tourists. Prior to the civil war, tourists contributed approximately 20 percent to Lebanon's GDP. After the war, it proved to be difficult to attract visitors. In the first eleven months of 2004, however, a record 1.2 million tourists traveled to Lebanon, whereas in past years, tourists had averaged only around 300,000. Tourism remained steady to Lebanon until 2005, when the assassination of Lebanon's former prime minister Rafiq al-Hariri raised some doubts as to whether Lebanon was truly the safest country in the Middle East. Doubts returned following the outbreak of the Syrian civil war in 2011, and tourism to Lebanon and the region is now at a record low.

Despite the economic downturn in the face of increased tensions in the region, Lebanon's banking industry continues to form a strong basis for its economy. In fact, some financial analysts have stated that the banking industry alone is responsible for Lebanon's continued—albeit slow—growth in recent years.

INTERNET LINKS

http://www.al-monitor.com/pulse/business/2016/05/lebanon-syria-war-economy-repercussions-banking-sector.html
This article from *Al-Monitor* looks at the consequences of the Syrian civil war on the Lebanese economy.

http://www.lebanonembassyus.org/the-economy.html
The Lebanese Embassy in the United States provides information about the largest sectors of the Lebanese economy.

ENVIRONMENT

The Qadisha Valley in Lebanon is a noted UNESCO World Heritage Site.

L EBANON HAS LONG SUFFERED FROM environmental degradation and abuse. Its legendary cedar forests were cut down as long ago as ancient Egypt, when they were used to build pyramids and palaces. The Romans and Turks also made use of Lebanon's abundant environmental resources. Of course, the more recent civil war led to a complete breakdown of government and caused greater environmental neglect, largely due to a lack of enforcement of environmental regulations and a lack of conservation efforts.

After the civil war, attention was focused on rebuilding Lebanon's cities and infrastructure, which meant that environmental concerns continued to be neglected. Since then, Lebanon has taken small steps to preserve and conserve its natural beauty. However, the Syrian civil war has brought new conflict into the region and, along with it, a large influx of refugees onto Lebanese territory. This crisis has once again put environmental concerns on the back burner for Lebanese officials and has, even more worryingly, stretched the natural resources that remain to the limit.

For many years, unregulated urban development and agriculture have harmed the cedar forests that Lebanon is known for. Over the past fifty years, 35 percent of Lebanon's forests have disappeared. Forest fires have contributed to this sad deterioration of the country's famous forests.

The Lebanese government has had to deal with the effects of air pollution in its capital in recent years.

AIR QUALITY

Air pollution is one of the greatest environmental threats facing the country. Because most Lebanese live in large cities—and some of these cities do not have functional transportation systems—they rely on private cars. For every one thousand people in Lebanon, there are almost five hundred cars. This large amount of vehicles on the road belch out noxious exhaust fumes, harming the environment as well as city residents' health. Before 2002, gasoline in Lebanon was sold with high levels of lead. However, a government initiative to phase out high-lead gasoline has been successful and has positively impacted air pollution.

Recent research, however, has shown that Lebanon's air quality remains below international standards. While attention to this issue and, thus, capabilities in air pollution monitoring have increased, the situation remains dire. Recent government directives to curb air pollution have included Environmental Law 341 to encourage the use of less-polluting fuels, although this law has only been partially enforced.

QUARRYING

Rebuilding Lebanon after its civil war required ample quarries from which rock and sand could be removed. Unfortunately, for a long time quarrying was not regulated in the country, which led to the destruction of wildlife habitats and natural vegetation, as well as many abandoned quarries. There are over seven hundred quarries in Lebanon, and many of them are abandoned. In 2003, a ban on quarrying was issued. However, this did not stop illegal quarrying. In 2015, truck drivers protesting the closing of quarries shut down many roads leading into and out of Beirut, stopping traffic and causing chaos. The quarry ban was subsequently deemed illegal, and some abandoned quarries have been reopened. This could have continued devastating consequences for the health of both animals and humans alike in nearby areas.

PESTICIDE USE

Excessive pesticide use has long been a problem in Lebanon. Fears of pesticide-laden produce reached a fever pitch in 2009, when studies on locally grown fruits and vegetables showed that some contained more than twenty-five times more pesticides and chemicals than international standards allowed. This began a campaign launched by the government to educate farmers on making sure their agricultural products are safe for consumption. However, testing done in 2013 indicated that pesticide use was again skyrocketing.

Following a study, in 2013 the Lebanese government determined that pesticide use had skyrocketed in recent years.

There is a continued need for the Ministry of Agriculture to reach and advise farmers on correct agricultural practices. There are campaigns under way, however, to promote awareness of the dangers of pesticide overuse. Over the past twenty years, the total use of fertilizers has decreased as farmers have learned alternatives to chemical pesticides and fertilizers. Voluntary organizations have also taken it upon themselves to monitor the safe and effective use of agrochemicals.

WATER POLLUTION

Large numbers of people and factories have polluted the Mediterranean Sea to an extreme degree. Garbage and sewage is often dumped into the sea, not just from Lebanon but also from all countries surrounding the Mediterranean. According to some experts, militias during the Lebanese civil war allowed the dumping of toxic waste along Lebanon's shore by European countries in exchange for money. As a result, open dumps continue to dot the Lebanese coastline.

This has had devastating results. The surface water is often covered with small particles of raw sewage, which sometimes gather into ugly masses of yellow muck. The few patches of unpolluted beach near Beirut that have survived are now the domain of private resorts, which charge for admission.

UNREGULATED DEVELOPMENT

As in other sectors, unregulated building has become a cumbersome problem in Lebanon. Little government oversight exists in these building projects, launched particularly along the coast and in north Beirut, which often continue with little regard to wildlife habitat, safety, or preserving natural landscapes or important historic sites. In 2010, the United Nations Educational, Scientific, and Cultural Organization (UNESCO) warned that Lebanon's Qadisha Valley, a world heritage site due to the ancient monasteries that dot its landscape, would be in danger of being dropped from their list because of uncontrolled building and development, as well as pollution and sewage. Oftentimes, unregulated

Early Christian monasteries—side by side with modern dwellings—dot the hills of the Qadisha Valley.

buildings are built too close to one another, with little or no provision for sewage treatment. Little has been done by the government to curb this problem, which can have health risks such as promoting infectious diseases.

A POLLUTED WATER TABLE

Since the civil war, the Lebanese government has struggled to deal with its water resources. Shelling during the war polluted both the water table and natural springs throughout the country. In order to get potable water, many Lebanese had no choice but to dig their own wells, which would quickly become polluted, too. It is estimated that over twenty thousand illegal groundwater wells exist just in the region of Beirut and Mount Lebanon. This is because drinking water remains unavailable to many Lebanese except for a few hours a day, and the water they do get is often unsanitary and unsafe for drinking.

In recent years, the Lebanese government has tried to address this problem. The Greater Beirut Water Supply Project began in 2010, with partial funding from the World Bank. This project will eventually provide 8,828,666 cubic feet (250,000 cubic meters) of water every day to Beirut and its surrounding regions. A water treatment plant south of Beirut will treat water to international standards. In addition, large dam projects are underway around the country in order to increase the volume of water stored, treated, and made available for use.

CONSERVATION

According to a 2010 World Bank report, the cost of environmental degradation in Lebanon is estimated to be $565 million a year, or 3.4 percent of its GDP. This number has likely increased since 2011 with the influx of refugees in the country and the cost of war in the region. Because of continued weak government control in the implementation of environmental measures, the population has suffered from preventable diseases and even premature death.

It is therefore encouraging that Lebanon recognizes the value of conservation. This is seen most clearly in the establishment of a Ministry of Environment in 1993 and in the growing number of environmentalist

Recycling bins, such as these, have been placed throughout larger cities and towns in Lebanon.

groups like Green Line, a voluntary organization promoting awareness and conservation of the environment.

Since 1992, Lebanon has declared eight nature reserves, twelve forests, and several river basins and mountains as being protected areas. In addition, the Green Plan Project was initiated to control soil erosion and to prohibit animals, particularly goats and sheep, from grazing on protected areas. The Ministry of Agriculture has joined in these efforts. It has banned tree logging and can punish violators with a fine and a jail term.

Although little was done to encourage waste reduction, efforts have been directed into recycling. A community waste and collection program by the Center for the Environment and Development was established, teaching the public how to convert used items into useful products. Schools have also initiated recycling campaigns. Between 1995 and 1997, 75,000 tons (68,000 metric tons) of paper were collected and recycled. Sukleen, a private waste management company, has placed containers for glass, plastic, and metal around Beirut, where residents can sort their waste for recycling. In Lebanon there are at least five companies that recycle paper, four for glass, and a few others for recycling metal and plastic. The Ministry of Environment is also investigating ways to reduce Lebanon's dependency on plastic shopping bags.

Promoting Lebanon as an ecological destination for hikers not only promotes tourism but also helps disseminate information on Lebanon's environmental concerns. Such an increase in environmental awareness bodes well for the nation's fragile environment.

ENVIRONMENTAL TREATIES

In the wake of civil crisis and economic devastation, the Lebanese government has often put economic concerns above environmental ones. However,

Lebanon has signed and ratified eighty-one environmental treaties, including the United Nations Convention to Combat Desertification in 1996. This treaty paved the way to begin greater protection of Lebanon's forests. The Ramsar Convention, signed in 1999, focused on protecting Lebanon's wetlands and conserving and sustaining its biodiversity.

Since 1993, Lebanon has agreed to phase out emissions of greenhouse gas as ratified in the Montreal Protocol and agreed to refrain from adding to Earth's rising temperature as a party to the Convention for Ozone Layer Protection. In 1994, Lebanon ratified the Basel Convention on minimizing the amount of waste generated and the sound management of hazardous waste and also ratified the Convention on Climate Change to set emission limits on greenhouse gas in order to avoid interfering with the natural climate system.

In addition to ratifying the UN Convention on the Law of the Sea, which includes dealing with pollution of the marine environment, Lebanon is also a party to the Marpol Convention on preserving the marine environment

The Ramsar Convention was signed in 1999 to protect Lebanon's many wetlands.

The Palm Islands Reserve is small but protects many endangered flora and fauna.

by eliminating dumping oil and other harmful pollutants into the sea. Treaties on environmental modification and marine life conservation have been signed but not ratified.

AL SHOUF CEDAR RESERVE

Lebanon's largest nature preserve was established in 1997 and now occupies 5 percent of the country's total land area. It covers 123,000 acres (49,778 ha) of cedar forests, wetlands, mountain ranges, and prairies, and 25 percent of Lebanon's remaining cedar forests lie in its boundaries. The reserve is home to 250 bird species, 520 species of plants, and 31 species of reptiles and amphibians, among other animals, including wolves and gazelles.

PALM ISLANDS RESERVE

Three rocky, limestone islands—Ramkine, Sanani, and Palm Island—make up this important reserve, which lies to the west of Tripoli. Although small, with a total area of 3 square miles (8 sq km), it protects many endangered animals, including Mediterranean monk seals, rare sea sponges, marine turtles, and migratory birds.

Established in 1992, the Palm Islands Reserve is a designated Mediterranean Specially Protected Area under the Barcelona Convention, an Important Bird Area by Birdlife International, and a Wetland of Special International Importance. In the summer months, parts of the reserve are open to the public for snorkeling and swimming.

TYRE BEACH RESERVE

This small reserve was established in November 1998, just south of Tyre at Ras al-Ain. The reserve is cut in half by the Rachidiye refugee camp, and is

The government, volunteer organizations, and private entrepreneurs have made much effort to conserve and protect what remains of Lebanon's trees and wildlife. Funding from various local and international private organizations, as well as the government, has made it possible to run these nature reserves. The Ministry of Environment is the guardian of Lebanon's nature reserves.

made up of two zones: one for conservation and one for recreation. Three springs provide freshwater habitats for sea creatures, and a sandy beach provides sanctuary for endangered turtles, birds, and other wildlife. It is an important nesting site for the loggerhead and green sea turtle, as well as the Arabian spiny mouse and the European badger.

INTERNET LINKS

http://greenline.me.uk
The Green Line Association website provides information about their current campaigns for environmental protection.

http://www.moe.gov.lb/ProtectedAreas/tyre.htm
The Lebanese Ministry of the Environment gives information about protected areas, including Tyre Beach Reserve, on their website.

LEBANESE

Lebanese friends display their painted hands during a festival in Beirut.

LEBANON STANDS AT THE CROSSROADS of many cultures—and so, too, do the Lebanese. The Lebanese today can claim a vast range in ancestry, largely due to the mixture of peoples—including the Phoenicians, Greeks, European Crusaders, and Arabs—who at different times occupied and populated the country.

But the Lebanese identity itself is relatively new. Lebanon only defined itself as a separate country following World War I. Prior to this, people in the area thought of themselves first as Ottoman citizens, and then identified themselves by the region in which they lived. Then, when civil war broke out in 1975, identities were once again divided. Residents identified themselves first by their religion before stating that they were Lebanese. Only in the 1990s did a national identity begin to coalesce again and Lebanese citizens identified themselves as such.

ETHNICITY

While it is difficult to say with certainty due to the lack of recent census data, over 90 percent of the population is ethnically Arab, including both Muslims and Christians. This shared ethnic heritage is largely due to the Arabization process that began during the seventh century CE. However, some Christians prefer to call themselves Phoenicians in order to bring attention to the ethnic history of the country before Arabization. This is very much a political identity, as most Lebanese have shared ethnic

6

Today, the notion of identity is still fraught in Lebanon. Some Lebanese Christians prefer to call themselves Phoenicians to distinguish themselves from Arab Muslims. Due to the political sensitivity of the country's religious demographics, no official census data on ethnicity has been collected since 1932.

Young Lebanese students catch up on the steps of the American University of Beirut.

The last official census in Lebanon was taken in 1932. No other official censuses have been conducted due to tensions between religious and ethnic groups.

heritage, and it is a way of focusing on Christian or pre-Islamic heritage.

In a country that has been torn apart by a civil war for over fifteen years, it is not surprising that people have conflicting ideas about how they want to define themselves. Indeed, the whole question of how many Lebanese actually belong to each of the different religious groups is a highly controversial matter.

The largest ethnic minority are the Armenians, who make up 4 percent of the population. They arrived in Lebanon in the early twentieth century, escaping massacres in Turkey. In 1924, they were granted citizenship by the French, who wanted to increase the number of Christians in the country. The Armenians have their own language and culture, and they tend to live together in their own communities in the cities. Like Armenians in other parts of the world, they welcomed the creation of an independent Armenia east of Turkey in 1991.

Assyrians are an ethnic minority group that fled from Iraq in the early decades of the twentieth century and, later, from Syria in the 1950s. They are all Christians. There is an equally small number of Kurds, less than 1 percent of the population. Being Muslims, they have been absorbed into the Arabic culture of the country.

Palestinians are another group of non-Lebanese Arabs living in the country. Many of their ancestors fled from Israel. Most Palestinians now live in camps that often lack basic amenities. Since the Syrian civil war began in 2011, approximately 1.5 million Syrian Arab refugees have entered Lebanon and are living in these refugee camps as well.

CONFESSIONALISM

Lebanon's political system is organized around confessionalism, which divides political representation based on confessional communities. Confessional communities are groups of people who identify mainly not through national identity or ethnicity but through their religious affiliation. The idea is that confessional communities can have a larger power of representation in the government if they band together for similar social, political, and economic needs.

Today, all Lebanese citizens are required to carry an identity card that states which confession they belong to. This does not mean that an individual practices a religion—for example, that a Christian Lebanese attends church regularly, or a Muslim Lebanese regularly goes to prayer at a mosque. These confessional categories have more political than religious significance and influence the country's governance.

All Lebanese citizens must carry around identity cards, which state whether they are Christian or Muslim, or whether they belong to another religion.

ARABS

While many Arabs practice Islam across the Middle East and define themselves by their religion, the Lebanese tend to be an exception. Lebanon is a predominantly Arab society in terms of language and culture, but many Arab Lebanese are Christian. They speak Arabic and share in an Arab culture common to the whole country. This is very unusual in an Arab society and has given Lebanon a reputation for the special mélange of its culture.

Arabs were the original people who lived in the Arabian Peninsula, where Islam was born. As the religion spread, so too did the Arabic language, and the term "Arab" came to represent all those who speak Arabic. Consequently, not all Arabs look alike, and the color of their skin and hair varies widely from light to dark. The Arabs of Lebanon look very much like the Arabs of neighboring Middle Eastern countries and are usually dark-haired with lightly tanned skin.

DRUZE

The Druze follow an Islamic sect that also incorporates ancient elements of Judaism, Christianity, Gnosticism, and Greek philosophy. The oldest Druze

The Druze form an important confessional group within Lebanon.

communities in the world are located around Mount Lebanon and in the south of Syria. While the Druze have been historically persecuted by different governments and religious groups, they also have assimilated successfully into their countries. As Arabic speakers who share the same social customs as other religious groups in Lebanon, the Druze are virtually indistinguishable from other Lebanese. The only thing that separates the Druze from other Lebanese is their religious beliefs, and their closely guarded theology has made them form close-knit communities based on these shared beliefs. Like Muslims, the Druze do not drink alcohol. However, unlike Muslims, the Druze believe in reincarnation.

MARONITE CHRISTIANS

The Maronite sect is the largest group of Christians in Lebanon. Maronites mainly come from the region around Mount Lebanon and follow the teachings of the Christian saint Maron. Maronites have lived in the country since the fifth century CE and have had historically close ties with France and French culture. Many Maronites speak French fluently and adopt French names. While many Maronites remain in Lebanon, Maronites emigrated from their country beginning in the early twentieth century and have formed large communities in Europe, South and Central America, and North America.

PALESTINIAN REFUGEES

Many Palestinians fled their homes south of Lebanon in 1948 when the state of Israel was created and ended up north, in Lebanon. The United Nations Relief and Works Agency for Palestine Refugees (UNRWA) was created to look after Palestinian refugees in Lebanon and to build camps on the outskirts of Beirut and other large towns. During the first five years, refugees were registered and entitled to free education and health care, as well as other benefits. However, this provision came to an end in the early 1950s. Since then, most Palestinian refugees have kept their refugee status and have never been naturalized; this means that they receive no government benefits and have no political representation in government.

Today, over half the registered Palestinians still live in camps, often with very poor living conditions, and they face disadvantages in nearly all aspects of life. It is estimated that within the refugee camps there are over twelve different factions, and most Palestinians have no choice but to yield to the authority of whatever faction happens to control their area. They are also barred from working in most professions, further hindering their ability to survive in Lebanon.

During the first half of the civil war, from 1975 to 1982, Palestinians in Lebanon were heavily involved in fighting against the Christian groups. They paid a terrible price for this in 1976 when Christian militias in Tel-el-Zaater murdered some 2,500 Palestinian men, women, and children. More massacres took place in Shatila and Sabra in 1982 under cover of invading Israeli troops.

Today, over four hundred thousand Palestinians—or about 6 percent of the population of Lebanon—have no hope of citizenship either in Lebanon or in a new Palestinian state. The refugees living in camps at Shatila and Sabra have been attacked and massacred on more than one occasion. The camps were last flattened in 1985 after a long siege by Shiite militias. Both camps have been shelled and rebuilt a number of times.

The camps were initially scheduled to be pulled down permanently. The government, as part of its ambitious plan to rebuild Beirut, wished to construct a new sports stadium on the land occupied by fifty thousand Palestinians. The demolition did not happen, however, as the stadium was rebuilt on land adjacent to the camp.

Many refugees living in Lebanon are not granted the full rights that Lebanese citizens enjoy.

Even thirty years after the civil war, the Lebanese struggle to cope with the trauma of the war that left 150,000 dead and 75,000 with permanent disabilities. Over half a million people left the country during the fighting.

MILITIAS

A young Lebanese soldier holds his rifle along the country's border with Israel.

During the civil war, a familiar stereotype of a young Lebanese man armed with lethal weapons and dressed in military uniform was propagated. This is because many young men who felt demoralized or ostracized—and usually came from economically disadvantaged families—became enticed by the stated goals of different militias that formed throughout the 1970s and 1980s. These militias were typically religious power groups, organized to gain political power for a particular religion and group. In addition to national armies, by the mid-1980s, there were almost twenty different militia groups operating in Lebanon. Most of these groups were operated by young Lebanese, sometimes in their teens or early twenties.

The motives that led even boys in their early teens to drop out of school and join the militias were not always clear-cut. It was not uncommon that these young men did not even know what their militia stood for. What they did see was an economic opportunity (members of militias were paid a regular wage), the offer of protection from rival militias, and a sense of belonging and power. These factors often played a more important role than politics. The grim reality was their easy access to arms and the frequent use of them. Teachers, for example, were sometimes threatened by armed students or militia soldiers.

When the main opposition to the Taif Agreement was defeated in October 1990 and the civil war ended, the militias slowly disbanded and put down arms, with the exception of Hezbollah, which provides unofficial military defense in south Lebanon.

LEBANESE AROUND THE WORLD

Due to famine and war, there is a long history of different groups of Lebanese people migrating to other countries. This is called a diaspora, meaning the spread of an ethnic group beyond the borders of its own territory.

The earliest generation of Lebanese migrants was mostly male and largely Christian. Many worked as peddlers. Such a job required very hard work but little capital, and from such humble beginnings, many Lebanese established successful lives far from the eastern Mediterranean. As early as the first decade of the twentieth century, it was estimated that over 40 percent of Lebanon's foreign earnings came from money sent home by Lebanese abroad. The successful emigrant often returns to Lebanon to retire.

Before the civil war, there were about one million Lebanese nationals living overseas, and most of them were Christians. During the civil war, the number of people leaving the country increased, and both Muslims and Christians left. Between 1975 and 1987, well over half a million people—mostly professionals or semiskilled laborers—left the country. At some point during the civil war in Lebanon, nearly one in four Lebanese were living abroad. In 2013, the Lebanese diaspora abroad numbered about fourteen million.

People leave Lebanon primarily for economic reasons. They go to countries where there are employment possibilities. The United States, Brazil, Australia, and the United Kingdom have always been popular destinations, but in recent years the oil-rich states of the Middle East have attracted increasing numbers of Lebanese.

One of the earliest Arab American autobiographies published in the United States is called *Syrian Yankee*, written by the Lebanese writer Salom Rizk in 1943. This book fictionalizes Rizk's own struggle moving to the United States and integrating into American culture.

INTERNET LINKS

http://joshuaproject.net/people_groups/11620/LE
The Joshua Project website gives detailed information about the Druze and their lives today in Lebanon.

http://www.psc.isr.umich.edu/research/tmp/moaddel_lebanese_survey_pr_jan08.pdf
This academic paper by Mansoor Moaddel examines the religious beliefs and ethnical identification of the contemporary Lebanese.

LIFESTYLE

Just like many people around the world, Lebanese enjoy socializing outside the home in restaurants, clubs, and

7

THE LEBANESE PRIDE THEMSELVES on continuing to live despite the ravages of constant war. For many years, going down the street to buy groceries in Beirut meant taking one's life in one's hands. But this didn't stop the Lebanese from living—and from enjoying life. As one Lebanese woman puts it, "Even during the shelling, people went shopping. The Lebanese are like this. We like to live."

Indeed, the Lebanese are known not just for their love of life but also for their love of beauty and luxury. Many Lebanese, although they only earn an average salary of approximately $4,500 per year, don't hesitate to buy luxury international goods from brands like Christian Dior and Yves Saint Laurent, which could cost a large percentage of their annual salary. For some foreigners, this might seem frivolous, but for the Lebanese, this is a real survival strategy focused on living in the moment and enjoying the finer things in life while the opportunity exists.

RECOVERY

Although the civil war ended over twenty-five years ago, it still plays a large role in the daily lives of many Lebanese, along with other conflicts that have erupted since then. Many Lebanese alive now lost friends and loved ones during the conflicts. They still bear scars—psychological or

The postwar administration in Lebanon agreed to give general amnesty for all political crimes perpetrated during the civil war before 1991. Many Lebanese have widely criticized this choice and feel that it has contributed to further divisions and small-scale conflicts.

A traditional small farmhouse in the Lebanese countryside

otherwise—from the troubles they have been forced to endure.

In many cases during the long war, people had to abandon their homes at short notice and returned months or years later to find the shattered remains. "We were the last to leave. It was the middle of the night, and our neighbors came and knocked on the door, shouting urgently that we had to go; we could hear guns very close. We left with nothing. If we'd been able to take things with us, we would have been all right. But we left with nothing and now we've come back with nothing. We thought we'd be gone a few weeks or months. It has been ten years now." These words of a man from south Lebanon were spoken as he laid some new bricks on a broken wall of his old home. When the wall was repaired, he planned to begin work on his garden.

All over Lebanon, people continue to rebuild their homes, and indeed their lives, following the conflicts they have endured. Conflicts in the south of the country have driven some Lebanese farther north, to cities like Beirut or Tripoli. The cost of living in Lebanon is high, and housing, if available at all, is expensive. This is why most Lebanese go to the capital, as it offers the best chance of employment. On weekends and during occasional holidays, families leave the capital and return to their villages for a working holiday.

REMAINING SCARS

During the war, buildings were not the only things that were destroyed by constant conflict—relationships also took a big hit. This was because groups of people who had lived together for many centuries in peace often were faced with choosing a side in the war based on their religious affiliation and the dictates of their family. It took many years for the anger and resentment that bubbled during the war to be repaired.

Many villages once had clusters of Christians and Muslims living side by side. The civil war polarized relationships, and neighbors fought neighbors. Friends became enemies overnight. Rebuilding a friendship is not always as easy as rebuilding a house because bitter memories remain. After the civil war, political flare-ups in the country could lead to continued divisions. While the war ended over twenty-five years ago, scars still remain.

There is, surprisingly, a positive side to the hardship caused by the years of fighting. In many instances, people joined together to help their neighbors when they all faced the challenge of survival in terribly harsh conditions. In doing this, they were following the age-old custom of friendly solidarity. The Lebanese have many traditional sayings that reflect the importance of being neighborly, including "Joy is for all, and mourning is for all" and "The neighbor who is near is more important than the brother who is far."

The Martyrs' Statue in Beirut honors those who lost their lives during the country's civil war.

ECONOMIC DIVISIONS

As in many countries around the world, Lebanon's society is becoming vastly divided based on economic standing and opportunities. Recent studies have shown that the number of Lebanese living below the poverty line has increased by 66 percent since 2011 and that approximately 350,000 Lebanese live on less than $1 a day. For refugees living in Lebanon, however, these statistics are even more dire.

A survey of the quality of life in one of the refugee camps near Tyre, for example, revealed appalling conditions. Sewage as well as contaminated

Population: *6 million (2016 estimate)*

Birth rate: *14.4 births per 1,000 of the population (2016 estimate)*

Death rate: *4.9 deaths per 1,000 of the population (2016 estimate)*

Life expectancy: *76.3 years for men; 78.9 for women (2016 estimate)*

Literacy rate: *93.9 percent over the age of 15 can read and write (2015 estimate)*

Unemployment rate: *24 percent (2016 estimate)*

water are just some of the problems that the refugees have to live with. Daily food rations from UN relief funds are the only source of comfort for many refugees. Others have to compete with Syrian guest workers for a chance to do menial labor for very low pay. Today in Lebanon, over 55 percent of all private income goes to one-fifth of the population. The poorest one-fifth of the country, on the other hand, lives on only 4 percent.

Affluence is often open and ostentatious, particularly in the cities. Apartments of the rich are well stocked with appliances, there are many cars on the roads, and children are given music lessons and go to good schools.

Before the war, everything the rich could afford was found in the city center, particularly in Beirut: movie theaters, first-class shops, and good schools and colleges. Encircling the city were the living quarters of the poor and the factories where they worked.

The majority of citizens work very hard trying to maintain a decent life on meager wages, threatened constantly by inflation. The upheavals of the last forty years have accelerated the migration of people from the countryside into Beirut, aggravating the already overcrowded and poverty-stricken existence of the poor.

YOUTH

While the youth in Lebanon are typically well educated, young men and women between the ages of eighteen and thirty-five are experiencing the worst levels of unemployment in years. As of 2016, total unemployment in Lebanon stands at 24 percent, while nearly 35 percent of the Lebanese youth cannot find a job. This is among the highest unemployment rate not only in the world but in the whole Middle East and North Africa (MENA) region besides in those areas besieged by war. The vast majority of all those who are unemployed hold university degrees, but cannot find work regardless of their education.

This inconsistency can be attributed to a few factors. The education system in Lebanon, as in many Arab countries, has dual features. For example, the system is either secular or religious, the subject of study either general or technically specific, and the language taught and used is either native or foreign. With such variance, even highly educated youth may not be able to find suitable employment if their skills and knowledge do not correspond to the needs of the job market. As a result, many have to find employment outside their field of study. The practice of cronyism by potential employers is another reason for the high unemployment rate. Suitable candidates for a job may be bypassed in favor of an employer's less qualified acquaintance. It is thus not surprising that Lebanon is facing a brain drain, as almost three hundred thousand youth are emigrating to greener pastures every year.

In 2010, Lebanon's parliament rejected a bill to reduce the voting age for youth from twenty-one to eighteen years old. This somewhat limits youth participation in Lebanon's political scene. Further, schools and universities play limited roles in supporting political aspirations. However, it is an encouraging fact that many young people have engaged in organized social activities and workshops over the past few years and are exposed to such aspects of political awareness as human rights, environment, and human welfare. With these experiences, it is hoped that they will actively cultivate their inclinations toward good governance.

The Lebanese education system varies greatly depending on whether it is a public or religious school.

WOMEN'S STATUS

While many women in Lebanon—particularly those who live in large cities—experience more freedom in their lives than women who live in other countries in the Middle East, the Lebanese legal system continues to discriminate against women. Lebanese women can dress as they choose and move freely without being accompanied by men, and they enjoy the same basic civil rights as Lebanese men. However, there are some worrying inconsistencies in legal practice. For example, a man who kills a wife, sister, or mother may avoid conviction if he can prove that the woman committed adultery. Marriageable age for women can be as young as nine years old, and polygamy is not outlawed. Also, only males may confer citizenship on their spouses and children. This means that if a woman is Lebanese and a man is a Palestinian refugee—meaning that he is legally "stateless"—children born to the couple will inherit the father's statelessness.

Religious groups have beliefs about a woman's role that may influence their laws concerning marriage and family property rights. Sometimes this means that there is discrimination against women. For example, a Sunni inheritance law gives a son twice the share of a daughter. It is also the case that a Muslim man may divorce easily, but a Muslim woman may do so only with her husband's agreement.

In many families, particularly those in rural areas, women and girls are still expected to manage all household chores, including washing, cooking, cleaning, and taking care of children or younger siblings. In urban areas, it is much more common for Lebanese women to be in the workforce and earn a living for themselves and their families. However, as of 2014, only 26 percent of working-age women were in the labor force in Lebanon, compared with 76 percent of Lebanese men. While this percentage remains low, it represents an increase of nearly 10 percent from ten years earlier. About 70 percent of Lebanese women in the workforce work in banking, finance, trade, and tourism. Women continue to become highly educated in Lebanon and are becoming more active in politics. While there is still a long way to go, many other Arabs consider the Lebanese to be quite progressive in women's issues.

Henna is traditionally used to decorate the hands of those celebrating various special occasions.

COSMETICS

Lebanese women are known for their love of—and ample use of—cosmetics. In large cities like Beirut, Lebanese women often dress in strikingly fashionable outfits whether going to the grocery store or to work, and they often have their hair and makeup done. A more traditional form of cosmetic can also be used. Henna, a dye made from the leaves of the henna shrub, can be mixed from a powder into a paste and applied on hands and feet in complex patterns. These colorful red and brown designs are often worn for celebrations, such as weddings.

Most Lebanese women also use a sugary solution as a waxing lotion to remove unwanted hair. About one cup of sugar is mixed with half a cup of water and a small amount of fresh lemon juice. The mixture is boiled to make a concentrated syrup and then left to cool on a cold surface. Before it gets

A *liwan* is a room in a traditional Lebanese house that opens up to the outside through an arched doorway.

too cold, the lotion is applied to the skin as a thin layer, then peeled off in the opposite direction of hair growth.

CLOTHING

Many men and women wear Western clothes in the cities. Women do not feel pressured to cover themselves up in the cities and may wear shorts or revealing shirts. In the country, modest and traditional dress is more common. Sometimes women wear modest and colorful skirts in rural areas, while men wear the traditional *sherwal*, which look like baggy cotton pants. Outdoors, some Muslim women may choose to wear the veil or even the *niqab*, a garment that covers them from head to toe.

LIFE IN THE COUNTRY

Most Lebanese live in or around big cities, and only 12 percent live in rural areas. Of the total Lebanese workforce, approximately 10 percent work in agriculture—a relatively low percentage in the Arab world. In the countryside, dependence on extended family—for work, caretaking, and fun—is essential to daily life. As more people migrate into the cities, they bring with them this emphasis on the family network.

Most farms are very small, slightly more than 2 acres (less than 1 ha). They are owned by single families that cultivate the land, and because each farm is so small, the family income usually needs to be supplemented from another source. In the Bekáa Valley, the average farm size is larger, around

Family honor is very important and is expressed in various ways. Hospitality functions as a form of honor and is often extended to include a sense of responsibility for one's guest. A visitor to a Lebanese home is always treated graciously, and food is naturally offered as an expression of hospitality.

Visitors to the country are often surprised at the hospitality shown them. A social encounter with one friendly person can easily lead to visits from place to place to meet all the family members and close friends.

7 acres (2.8 ha), but the lack of rainfall restricts the types of crops that can be grown.

The traditional farmhouse includes a *liwan* (LEE-wan), a room that opens onto the outside through a large arched doorway. Such houses are traditionally built of dried mud and straw bricks because it costs too much to cart building stone in by truck. The flat roof of the house is covered with dried mud. During the hot summer months, the roof inevitably cracks and fractures. Most families have homemade ladders handy to reach the roof so they can carry out the necessary repairs.

Traditional rural clothing for women consists of a loose dress that reaches the ankles, while men wear loose trousers and large shirts. Such clothing suits the dry, hot climate.

LOYALTY TO FAMILY

Sectarianism continues to affect the values held by many Lebanese. This means that, rather than national affiliation, many Lebanese feel that loyalty to their religion and their family is more important. The reliance on family intensified during the prolonged civil conflicts, when family solidarity was the only reliable source of stability in the face of economic collapse and constant violence. In many extended families, members will pool their resources to fund the education of a younger relative, or will offer him or her to stay with them free of cost. Because there is no social security system in place, the

family structure is essential to caring for the ill and the elderly.

Honor is highly valued and is often more important than income. Among males, there is a macho element that is not very different from its counterpart in other cultures. It features a keen regard for male prowess and calls for vengeance to address a perceived insult.

EDUCATION

Compulsory education, which is free and provided by the government, runs from the age of six until fourteen. After the age of fourteen, it is no longer necessary to attend, and poorer students can drop out to find work in order to support their families. The Lebanese public education system mandates that math and science courses are taught either in French or in English. However, there is a much larger percentage of private schools in Lebanon than public schools.

Nearly all the secondary schools are funded by private religious groups. Parents who can afford to send their children to private secondary schools will usually also pay for a private primary education.

The prevalence of religious schools does, unfortunately, make it difficult to break down the religious divisions that have separated the Lebanese for so long.

Despite the lack of government-funded schools, the overall literacy rate remains one of the highest in the Middle East. The net primary school enrollment as of 2014 was 93 percent.

Many Christian Lebanese attend the University of Saint Joseph in Beirut.

CHRISTIAN SCHOOLS

Jesuits (members of a Roman Catholic religious order) arrived in 1625. Together with the Maronites, they established the first schools in Lebanon. In 1820, American Presbyterian missionaries landed in Beirut, and in 1866, they started what was to become the American University of Beirut. Protestant rivalry with Catholicism led to other schools being established by the Jesuits.

These schools taught in Arabic and revived the study of Arabic literature. The achievements of Arab civilization in the past were studied, and aided by Western notions of democracy, helped to kindle demands for political freedom from Ottoman rule.

The school year runs from October to June. Arabic is the major language of instruction. In many private schools, lessons are also taught in French or English. Some schools, like the French University of Saint Joseph in Beirut, caters more to Christians, and Muslim Lebanese are less likely to enroll.

INTERNET LINKS

http://education.stateuniversity.com/pages/827/Lebanon-EDUCATIONAL-SYSTEM-OVERVIEW.html
This website provides an in-depth view of the Lebanese educational system.

http://www.hrw.org/news/2015/01/19/lebanon-laws-discriminate-against-women
This Human Rights Watch report examines how women in Lebanon still face discrimination in the justice system.

RELIGION

A church and a mosque sit side by side on a street

8

LEBANON REMAINS A VERY DIVERSE country, not only in terms of ethnicity but also in terms of religion. About 54 percent of all Lebanese are Muslims, while 40 percent are Christians. About 5 percent of the population are Druze, who do not consider themselves to be Muslims.

Of course, this isn't the whole story. Within these major religions are many different sects and denominations. Lebanon's Muslim population is split equally between Shia and Sunni Islam, while the majority of Lebanese Christians—21 percent of the total population—belong to the Maronite Church. Following Maronite Catholics, 8 percent of the population identifies as Greek Orthodox, 5 percent Melkite Catholic, and 6 percent are a mixture of other Christian denominations. The remaining 1 percent of the population includes non-Christian minorities like the Baha'is and Jews. Given the wide range of religions and denominations, the way in which each group identifies itself and its relationships with other religious groups dictates the structure of the country's society as a whole.

ISLAM

Islam originated in modern-day Saudi Arabia in the early seventh century CE with the teachings of the Prophet Muhammad. Followers of the Prophet Muhammad and Islam's holy book, the Quran, are known as Muslims.

About 8 percent of the population of Lebanon are Greek Orthodox Christians, and they live mostly in Beirut, the southeast, and south of Tripoli. Byblos has the most significant Greek Orthodox population in Lebanon. According to the National Pact, the deputy speaker of parliament and the deputy prime minister must be Greek Orthodox Christians.

The religion is based on the observance of five pillars: the declaration of faith; the performance of prayers; the giving of alms; the observance of fasting; and the performance of the hajj, a pilgrimage to Mecca.

THE DECLARATION OF FAITH The declaration of faith, called the *shahada*, literally means "the testimony" in Arabic. The shahada is the Islamic creed and comprises one statement that all Muslims must state and believe: "There is no god but God and Muhammad is the messenger of God." In this way, believers can testify their faith before God. The shahada is recited upon births and deaths, and is a part of the five daily prayers that all Muslims must complete. Reciting the shahada is also the first and only formal step required when converting to Islam.

The Quran, the holy book of Islam, gives the names of twenty-eight prophets, of whom Muhammad was the last. Twenty-one of the prophets, including Jesus, are also mentioned in the Bible. Unlike in Christianity, where Jesus is given divinity as the son of God, Jesus is just one of the prophets in Islam. The scriptures of Abraham, the Torah of Moses, the psalms of David, and the gospels of the New Testament are also believed to be prophetic revelations of God.

DAILY PRAYER Muslims are called to pray at least five times a day: at dawn, noon, late afternoon, sunset, and night. The "call to prayer" is usually performed by a mosque official, the *muezzin*, who is selected for the beauty of his voice. Traditionally, the muezzin begins the call to prayer from the top of the minaret of a mosque, although today, these calls are usually prerecorded and broadcast through an amplifier.

Muslims can pray in a mosque, but this is not obligatory or always practical. Some public buildings have a small room reserved for prayers. Friday is the most holy day of the week, akin to the Christian Sunday, and on that day Muslim men will try to attend a mosque for their prayers. Women usually pray at home, but those who choose to pray at the mosque may do so in a section set aside for them.

Prayers begin by a ritual washing of the body to show one's willingness to be purified. Physical contact with a member of the other sex is not permitted until after prayers, and if a Muslim man accidentally touches a woman, he

THE SIXTH PILLAR OF ISLAM

Some Muslims say that the sixth pillar of Islam is jihad, which translates as "striving in the way of God." It is a much misunderstood term that is open to more than one interpretation. Consequently, its intention has been much argued about within the Islamic community.

It is often rendered in English as "holy war." Jihad can mean a holy war against the godless, but it also applies to a holy war by an individual against his or her own unholy instincts. In this latter sense, it has some similarity with the Christian idea of an individual's striving to be good and struggling with his or her own conscience.

must wash himself ritually once again before praying. The same goes for a woman if she accidentally touches a man.

The worshipper always prays in the direction of Mecca and makes a prearranged cycle of prayers. The prayers usually consist of passages from the Quran. Muslims prostrate themselves on a prayer mat in a series of different positions for each of the five daily prayers.

GIVING ALMS The third pillar of Islam is giving alms to the poor. Called *zakat*, alms-giving is obligatory once a Muslim has earned a certain minimum salary. Typically, 2.5 percent of a Muslim's earnings must be given to the poor. This is a reminder that, according to Islamic belief, all things ultimately belong to God. At certain times during the year, for example during the fasting month of Ramadan, charity should also be given, and even newborns are not exempted from this contribution. The religious authority appoints mosque officials to make this annual collection at the appropriate time.

FASTING Ritual fasting is obligatory during the month of Ramadan, which commemorates the first revelation of the Quran to the Prophet Muhammad. During this month, Muslims cannot consume any food or drink between sunrise and sunset. Muslims are also supposed to stay clean of other sins during this time and are prohibited from smoking during the fasting hours and thinking or speaking ill of others. Only those who are ill, menstruating,

Each year, millions of Muslims travel to Mecca and circumambulate the Kaaba.

pregnant or breastfeeding, or traveling are exempted from the fast, as well as children who have not reached puberty. Typically, when the sun sets, Muslim families have large, festive meals, and restaurants are open late to accommodate them.

PILGRIMAGE TO MECCA The pilgrimage to Mecca, in Saudi Arabia, is required for all Muslims who can afford to do it at least once in their lifetime. Called hajj, those who have completed the pilgrimage can be referred to by the honorary title of "hajj" for men or "hajja" for women. The pilgrimage includes circumambulating the Kaaba, or the holy center of Islam, and traveling seven times between Mount Safa and Mount Marwah in the Arabian desert.

Muslims make careful preparations for their pilgrimage, some as early as a year prior to leaving. Clearing all financial obligations and making sure their family members have been provided for are religious requirements. Special classes conducted by religious teachers coach would-be pilgrims in the rites, prayers, and rules. Pilgrims to Mecca dress in simple white unhemmed clothing called ihram (EE-ha-ram), meaning "godly raiment."

SHIISM

Shiism is a religious movement that began during the early days of Islam, following the death of the Prophet Muhammad. An argument between the Prophet Muhammad's followers over who would lead them after his death led to a break in early Islam. Those who believed that Ali, the son-in-law and cousin of the Prophet Muhammad, was the rightful spiritual leader became known as Shi'i (followers of Ali). This is usually Anglicized as Shiites.

The most important Shiite group is the "Twelver" Shiites, who believe that there were twelve holy men after Muhammad—Ali and his descendants. They believe that the twelfth holy man did not die and will return one day as savior of the world.

While the Druze do not permit iconography in their religion, they have a religious symbol known as the Druze Star. The Druze Star is a five-pointed star made of five colors: green, red, yellow, blue, and white. Each color refers to a metaphysical power that humans have that separates humans from animals. Green stands for intelligence, red for the soul, yellow for the ability to speak and communicate, blue for potentiality, and white for immanence.

In Lebanon, the Shiites tend to be the poorer citizens of the country and mostly share a farming background. In recent years, many Shiites have moved upward economically, becoming part of the middle class. Most of the world's Muslims are Sunni, and Shiites have experienced persecution in many Sunni-majority countries.

DRUZE

The Druze are an Islamic group that emerged in the eleventh century as a branch of Ismailism, a Shiite sect. However, the Druze do not consider themselves Muslim, despite this shared heritage. Shiites traditionally have been more mystical than their Sunni counterparts, and this mysticism found its way into early Druzism. The Druze believe in reincarnation, keep their central tenants secret to nonbelievers, and do not seek or accept converts. They believe, like Shiites, in *taqiyya*, which means concealing their beliefs when necessary to fit in with various communities.

The Druze believe that God has taken various incarnations as a living person on Earth, including that of Jesus Christ, and that he last took human form as al-Hakim in the eleventh century. The name of the religion is thought to derive from al-Darazi, a follower of al-Hakim.

Maronite Christians follow the teachings of Saint Maron.

Today there are about 2.3 million Druze worldwide and about 10 percent are in Lebanon. As a general rule, they marry only among themselves. They do not worship in a mosque but meet for prayers on Thursday evenings in a house close to their particular village.

SUNNI MUSLIMS

Over 80 percent of all Muslims in the world are Sunnis, although 50 percent of Lebanese Muslims follow Sunni Islam. Sunnis have traditionally been less persecuted around the world and their religion is less steeped in mystical beliefs than Shiites. They do not accept that Ali was the rightful successor of the Prophet Muhammad, although they do respect Ali and believe that he was a "rightly guided leader."

In Lebanon, the Sunnis traditionally are settled in the Mediterranean coastal cities of Beirut, Tripoli, and Sidon. Most of the Palestinian refugees in Lebanon are also Sunnis.

CATHOLICS

The largest Christian denominations in Lebanon—including Maronites, Greek Catholics, and Armenian Catholics—are all termed part of the Eastern Catholic Churches, which means that they accept and follow the authority of the pope in Rome although they practice their own rites.

The Greek Catholics are also called Melkites. They are the descendants of a Greek Orthodox community that broke off from the Greek Orthodox Church in the eighteenth century. They retain many of their Greek rites but accept the authority of the pope in Rome, which the Greek Orthodox Church members do not. Today, many Melkites live in the town of Zahlé.

The Armenian Catholics are distinguished by their usage of Greek in religious ceremonies. They came to Lebanon to escape the massacres of Armenians by the Turks around the time of World War I.

MARONITES

The Maronites form the majority of Christians in Lebanon. They are Catholics who traditionally lived in the northern part of the country, around Mount Lebanon, although they can also live in southern Lebanon today. The religious movement originated in Syria during the early seventh century CE before moving into Lebanon.

They take their name from Saint Maron, a fourth-century monk. Originally, the Maronites were monothelite, believing that Christ has one will but two natures, but in the twelfth century they grew closer to mainstream Roman Catholicism. They elect their own church leader, a patriarch, through their bishops, and if the bishops cannot agree on a choice within fifteen days, the pope in Rome makes an appointment.

In 1736, the Maronites became affiliated with the Roman Catholic Church, and this provided Catholic France with an excuse to ally itself with them in Lebanon. The Turkish government retaliated by supporting and encouraging the Druze, as a counterweight to France's influence. Today, the number of Maronites in Lebanon is estimated to be around nine hundred thousand. Traditionally, Maronites have identified themselves with the West, as they did in the time of the Crusades.

INTERNET LINKS

http://the-levant.com/shias-lebanon-history
Read this short history of the Shiites in Lebanon written for the *Journal of the Beirut Center for Middle East Studies*.

http://maronitemonks.org/wp/story-maronite-catholics
This website offers information on the history of the Maronite religion.

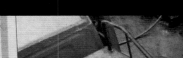

Lebanese newspapers are often printed in both Arabic and French.

9

WITH THE TYPICALLY LEBANESE mélange of ethnicities and religions, language use in Lebanon also shows the country's eclectic influences. Nearly all Lebanese speak and write Arabic. However, French is also widely spoken, particularly among Christian groups and the upper class. English is also a widely spoken language and is more important than French for international business. However, the influence of French is undeniable. In spoken Lebanese Arabic, for example, you will hear a smattering of French words melded with the Arabic.

ARABIC

Arabic is a Semitic language that developed in Arabia and was spread with Islam in the seventh and eighth centuries CE. Today, it is spoken by as many as 422 million people globally. Arabic is written from right to left, and short vowels are typically not marked in writing, which can make it difficult for non-native learners to read.

Arabic is a Semitic language, like Hebrew, that evolved from Aramaic, the language spoken in the Middle East during the first century CE. Aramaic, in turn, evolved from the Phoenician language.

The Quran is written in classical Arabic, which differs from the Arabic spoken across Lebanon today.

Arabic has more than one form. The spoken form, as used by people in their everyday lives, is known as colloquial Arabic. The various Arabic-speaking countries each have their own forms of colloquial Arabic. A Lebanese speaks Arabic and so does an Egyptian, for example, but their Arabic is not identical, and the speakers cannot always easily communicate. The Lebanese speak in Levantine Arabic, a dialect strongly influenced by Syriac and Aramaic. Within Lebanon itself, Arabic dialects differ from region to region, with the Druze having the most distinct dialect. In the more remote mountainous regions in the eastern part of the country, there are local dialects that do not have a written form. These are used only for communication within the local group, affecting geographically small areas.

Classical Arabic is quite different. It is the language of the Quran and provides a common and shared written form for all Arabic speakers.

A third form of Arabic, the Modern Standard Arabic (MSA), is a mixture of the first two. In its spoken form it provides a shared language for all Lebanese and also facilitates communication between the Lebanese and other Arabs.

Arabic belongs to the diglossic languages, or languages with significant differences between spoken and written forms, and it is regarded as a difficult language to learn. Lebanese linguists are working on the compilation of a Lebanese dictionary, one that lists words by theme rather than in the traditional ordering system of Arabic that groups words according to their linguistic roots.

THE ST. SAVIOUR MONASTERY

In the hills just north of Sidon lies an ancient monastery that houses an impressive library of manuscripts. The St. Saviour Monastery holds over three thousand manuscripts, dating from the eleventh to the nineteenth centuries—a historical treasure trove. Today, the monastery's collection is considered one of the most important in the world and includes such treasures as the oldest Arabic Bible in existence, printed in 1591 in Rome.

Some of the manuscripts were written in Syriac, an ancient language related to Aramaic and considered to be the dialect spoken by Christ. Syriac scholars also wrote in Arabic, and between the eighth and thirteenth centuries they translated into Arabic the works of Aristotle and Plato. The texts in Arabic went to Spain (when the Arabs ruled Spain), where they were translated into Latin, thus providing a cultural foundation for the European Renaissance, between the fourteenth and seventeenth centuries.

The St. Saviour Monastery houses many ancient manuscripts in its library.

The St. Saviour library was established in 1711 by the visionary founder of the monastery, Bishop Aftimios Sayfi. Some of his monks were given the assignment of tracking down original manuscripts that were scattered around the eastern lands of the Ottoman Empire. They were sent out with funds to purchase manuscripts and in the event a sale could not be arranged, had the task of copying the entire manuscript so that a copy might be preserved in the monastery library. Without the work of the monks from the St. Saviour Monastery, many important documents would have been lost forever.

Today, the monastery's monks continue their work to preserve these priceless documents. In partnership with the University of St. John in Minnesota, they have begun to digitally archive all of their manuscripts. As of 2012, nearly two thousand documents had already been photographed and preserved.

A POLITICAL STATEMENT

Language is not just a vehicle for communication in Lebanon; it is a political statement. A person's choice of language typically shows others who he or she is and can even allude to the person's political or religious stance. For

It often happens that Arabic words have more than one spelling when transliterated into English. For example, the Arabic musical instrument from which the European lute is derived appears in writing as both 'ud and oud, both pronounced in the same way (OOD). Another example is the religious group known both as the Druze and the Druse.

Transliteration from Arabic to English is difficult for two reasons: there are sounds in Arabic with no equivalent in English, and there are vowel sounds in spoken Arabic that do not appear in written Arabic. Because there is no agreed-upon system for transliteration, words regularly appear with different spellings.

"Habibi," when spoken to a male, or "habibiti," when spoken to a female, is a common term of endearment used in Lebanon. It literally means "my beloved," and is used between close family, friends, or lovers.

example, Muslim Lebanese often speak in Arabic to signify a link to their fellow Arabs, while some Christian Lebanese prefer speaking French to show their political opposition to Muslim groups and their affinity to Christian European groups. Sometimes choosing one language over another shows one's economic background, with more educated and wealthier individuals having been exposed to French and English.

Some Maronite groups would prefer schools to adopt the Lebanese colloquial dialect of Arabic instead of teaching classical Arabic. Those who have little sympathy for Arab nationalism perceive the use of classical Arabic as a tool of Arab nationalists. If Lebanon adopts its colloquial form of Arabic as the national language, it would be seen as distancing itself from the rest of the Arab world. This is very unlikely to happen.

Even names tend to signify one's religion in Lebanon. Popular Muslim names are Muhammad (also spelled Mohammed and Mohammad) and Ahmad, while French names like Pierre and Michel are likely to be chosen by Christians. Biblical names like Sarah may belong to either a Christian or a Muslim.

BODY LANGUAGE

Not all language is spoken. Gesturing and body language is a natural part of conversations all around the world and often convey shades of meaning that verbal language alone cannot. Common gestures found in Lebanon are similar to gestures found throughout the Arab world. In Lebanon, for example, a simple "no" can be expressed by raising one's eyebrows, tilting one's head, and making a "tsk tsk" noise. This is a common gesture across the Middle East, although in other parts of the world it may be misinterpreted as disapproval.

REPUPLIQUE LIBANAISE الجمهورية اللبنانية

Ministere De La Culture
Et De L,enseignement Superieur
Direction Generale Des Antiquites

وزارة الثقافة و التعليم العالي
المديرية العـامة للآثار

موقع اثار صور ـ المدينة

SITE ARCHEOLOGIQUE DE TYR_LA CITE

Many official signs across Lebanon are written in both Arabic and French.

Shaking the head from side to side does not mean "no," but "I do not understand." Stretching out a hand as if to open a door, while at the same time flicking the wrist and hand, can mean "What is the problem?" or "What do you want?" It often functions as a general expression of inquiry.

The right hand held over the heart usually means "No thank you." A traditional female greeting in Lebanon is raising the right hand and lightly touching one's chest. It is an Islamic gesture. Many younger Lebanese now simply greet each other with a handshake. In most social interactions, the right hand is used to give or receive anything. Men hold hands as a gesture of friendship or simple companionship. A male stranger asking for directions may be taken by the hand and shown the right direction.

INTERNET LINKS

http://www.omniglot.com/language/phrases/arabic_lebanese.php
The Omniglot website offers visitors a useful guide to common Lebanese Arabic phrases.

http://phoenicia.org/leblanguage.html
The Phoenicia website explains the difference between the Lebanese dialect of Arabic and the standard written form of Arabic.

ARTS

Ancient Greek–influenced statues are on display at the
National Museum of Beirut.

10

LEBANON HAS LONG BEEN KNOWN for its art scene—from its ancient monuments, to its position as the center of modern Arab thought, philosophy, and art in the twentieth century, to its thriving artistic movements today. In particular, Lebanese literature is widely acclaimed and can be found translated in many bookstores around the globe. Such writers as Kahlil Gibran, Hanan al-Shaykh, Rabih Alameddine, and Joumana Haddad are famous not only to Lebanese but to many readers around the globe. Lebanon is also known as a publishing center for Arabic-language texts and has hosted the International Arab Book Fair annually since 1956.

ANCIENT ART

Lebanese art reflecting the country's ancient heritage is treasured and is found not only within Lebanon but also in museums across the world. The National Museum in Beirut, the foremost archaeological museum

Archaeological evidence suggests that the flutelike *ney* has been played continuously for five thousand years, which makes it one of the oldest musical instruments in the world.

The palace at Beit ed-Din, some 30 miles (50 km) from Beirut, is the best example of nineteenth-century Lebanese architecture to be found anywhere in the country. It was built for the emir Beshir, who governed Lebanon for fifty years, and its construction took thirty years.

The palace is filled with porticoed courts, arcades, and fountains. The ceiling and walls were richly decorated by the best craftsmen in the country, using tiny pieces of mirror to create intricate mosaic designs in glass.

in the country, holds an especially rich collection of ancient art. Its collection ranges from artifacts from hunter-gatherer societies dating from 150,000 BCE, including pieces of pottery, to Bronze Age statuettes and Phoenician ceramics. The art from these different periods reflects changing influences, from the influence of Egyptian art and culture in Phoenician jewelry to Greek influence in statues following the reign of Alexander the Great.

One of the most highly regarded objects in the National Museum is an eleventh-century BCE hand-carved sarcophagus made for the king of Byblos. The king is shown holding a lotus blossom and enthroned between two sphinxes, mythological monsters with human heads and lions' bodies. The sphinx originated in the East, probably in Egypt, and is commonly found in ancient art from the eastern Mediterranean region. What really makes the sarcophagus outstanding is a carved alphabetic inscription that is one of the very earliest appearances of writing in the world.

BAALBEK Baalbek (sometimes written Baalbeck) is an ancient town located in the Bekáa Valley, east of the Litani River near the Anti-Lebanon Mountains. It has become famous for its ancient ruins and, in particular, its temples.

Temples were built originally in the early Bronze Age and were developed under Greek influence until at least the first century CE. During the seventh century, Muslim armies occupied these temples as a military base and built on top of the existing Greek ruins. A temple to the Greek god Dionysus (called Bacchus by the Romans) is one of the most well preserved Roman temples in the world. Ironically, it was preserved by this development by Islamic forces, which kept the temple's origin secret for many years.

The city of Baalbek is known for its ancient ruins, including the Temple of Dionysus.

The Dionysus temple has magnificent stately columns built from gigantic blocks of locally quarried stone, measuring 62 feet by 14 feet by 11 feet (19 by 4 by 3 m). The builders of Baalbek also used pillars of rose granite imported from Egypt. It has been estimated that it took some three years for the granite to be transported and erected at Baalbek.

Delicate sculptures in Baalbek depict lines of twining vines and other plants, including poppies and wheat. There is a sculpture of the Greek sun god, Helios, from which the town's earlier name, Heliopolis, or "city of the sun" came about (not to be confused with the Heliopolis of ancient Egypt).

ARCHAEOLOGY Following the civil war, a multibillion-dollar rebuilding project in Beirut has unearthed many ancient artifacts across the modern city. Unfortunately, ruins were demolished during the chaos of early building. However, for the past twenty years, fifty archaeologists have worked to save and recover these ancient finds. By forging relationships with developers before development begins, this team has saved numerous pieces of ancient Lebanese history, including a Phoenician neighborhood and an enormous Roman wall that occupies much of downtown Beirut.

The Phoenician neighborhood being excavated includes six houses where fishermen once lived. The narrow streets and arches that they used are still intact in places. Over the top of this Phoenician settlement, the Ottomans

An archaeologist examines a skeleton in an archaeological site north of Beirut.

also built homes. Between 1993 and 1996, a stretch of Ottoman wall 200 feet (60 m) long was among the archaeological finds, along with tombs, kilns for glass and pottery production, and mosaic floors from the Roman-Byzantine period.

The excavation work has also unearthed a treasure trove of antiquities from ancient Roman times: statues, glassware, a whole stretch of road still bearing the marks left by chariot wheels, and a bath that has now been partially restored. An inscription on a mosaic has been discovered with the following observation: "Jealousy is the worst of all evils. The only good about it is that it eats up the eyes and heart of the jealous."

TRADITIONAL INSTRUMENTS

Traditional instruments used in classical Lebanese and Middle Eastern music include a flutelike instrument called the *ney* (NAY). Archaeological evidence suggests that the ney has been played continuously for five thousand years, which makes it one of the oldest musical instruments in the world. Although the ney looks simplistic, consisting of a metal or plastic tube with six holes on one side and one on the other, it is deceptively difficult to play. Only very accomplished musicians can actually play the entire three-octave range of the instrument. Traditional musicians also play a drum called the *daff* (DAHF), which resembles a tambourine. Another tambourine-like instrument is the *riq* (reek).

The musical instrument with the most ancient lineage is the oud. It dates back at least five thousand years and is regarded as the forerunner of the European lute. The oud is the most important musical instrument in Arab culture, and there are a number of slightly different types. It is played with a plectrum (pick) or with the fingers of both hands.

Marcel Khalife became an important folk musician during the Lebanese civil war.

CONTEMPORARY MUSIC

Different forms of music, including contemporary rock, are well appreciated by the Lebanese. However, the country also has a strong tradition of folk music, and children are taught this musical style from an early age. Pop, heavy metal, and new musical fusions combining Arabic and Western arrangements are also increasingly popular.

When car bombings and kidnappings were regular events in Beirut, the lyrics of fusion musician Marcel Khalife reflected this highly charged political atmosphere. He wrote songs that dealt with experiences common for many Lebanese—being interrogated by border guards, for example. His music was regarded with suspicion by many politically powerful officials. To the ordinary people of war-torn Lebanon, however, he was a folk hero who lifted their despair into poetry, often reducing his audiences to tears.

His album *Jadal* is a quartet for two ouds, a riq, and a bass guitar. Khalife has also composed works for philharmonic orchestras, citing thirteenth-century Arab historians who wrote about ensembles composed for up to one hundred musicians. His favorite instrument is the oud.

Arabic pop music first came out of Cairo in the 1970s. It was initially deemed as being one dimensional because of repetitive vocals and the use of only one sound apparatus, the synthesizer. Twenty years later, pop music had evolved, and pianos, guitars, and drums became part of Lebanese pop music. Majida al-Rumi and Diana Haddad are among the more well-known pop music artists. The 4 Cats, Lebanon's first all female pop group, melds Arab and Western pop. Their first album, *Tic-Tick*, sold more than one million copies and stayed at number one on the Arabic top charts for more than four months.

FOLK DANCE

Traditional folk dance is important to Lebanese culture—the most important folk dance being the *dabke* (DAHB-key). This energetic five-step folk dance has ancient origins, dating back at least to Phoenician culture. It is performed in various forms throughout the Levant, including in Syria and

The *dabke* is the most important folk dance in Lebanon.

Palestine. This joyous dance is performed at celebrations, particularly weddings and baptisms, although it can also be performed spontaneously at small family parties. In 2011, a Lebanese group set a world record when a human chain of 5,050 dancers performed the dabke.

Performances of the dabke provide increasingly rare opportunities to see people dressed in traditional Lebanese mountain garb. When the dance is performed by women, they wear kerchiefs on their heads and brightly colored skirts. The traditional music that accompanies the dance has a distinctive jaunty sound with haunting undercurrents. The dabke has a number of themes that allow for variations in the dance form. They are usually related to aspects of village life such as marriage and disputes over land. The dance was characteristically performed by villagers when the day's work was done.

Arabic calligraphy adorns this Lebanese-made jewelry.

Lebanon has its own unique dance troupe, called Caracalla. The troupe's performance combines elements of Oriental dance, opera, theater, drama, and even modern literature. They are wildly popular and can be seen performing at some of Lebanon's summer festivals.

Belly dancing, involving sinuous and sometimes vigorous movements of the hips and abdomen, is often performed by young women, both informally and at nightclubs.

TRADITIONAL ART

Traditional Lebanese folk art includes a wide range of practices and often mixes Lebanese cultural influences with the characteristics of art found in the Levant as well as the larger Arab world.

In carpet weaving, a well-established craft, the necessary skills and knowledge of time-honored motifs are passed down from one generation to another within a family. The themes and patterns for carpets reveal the influence of the Islamic world, being mainly nonfigurative and favoring abstract but colorful designs.

Nadine Labaki was born in Beirut in 1974. She directed her first film while still a student at university, and it won the Best Short Film Award at the Biennale of Arab Cinema in 1997. Labaki has since directed four more films and has starred in many movies. She is known for breaking taboos in regard to the depiction of women in Lebanese cinema.

Filigree ornamental work in fine gold wire is a specialty, an offshoot of the jewelry craft that Lebanon is famous for. The motifs found in jewelry designs betray a strong Turkish influence from the Ottoman period. Flowers, birds, and crescents made of semiprecious stones and diamonds are favorite designs.

Artisans who work with precious metals used to do their tool work outside their shops in the bazaar, or souk. Lumps of gold were "pulled" by two or three men, who attached the gold to another man's belt and then stretched the gold out as the man with the belt slowly turned in circles, producing the thin gold wire used in many ornaments.

In Lebanon, men customarily specialize in working with gold and metal inlay, and other jewelry. Women, usually those living in the countryside, tend to concentrate on embroidery work in linen, cotton, and lace, and on carpet weaving.

MOVIES AND THEATER

Lebanese films have been gaining worldwide acclaim in recent years with the success of such directors as Nadine Labaki, Ziad Doueiri, and Phillipe Aractingi. The popular Lebanese Film Festival, which solely promotes Lebanese movies for an international audience, began in 2001.

Lebanese cinema was made throughout the civil war as an eloquent testimony to the resilience of Lebanese culture. *Beirut, the Encounter*, a 1986 film directed by Borhan Alawiya, illuminated the political and religious divisions of a Shiite Muslim from the south and his girlfriend, an Eastern Christian. The film focuses on the potential of their love but their final inability to bridge the gaps that have torn apart their country.

Following the war, a lack of state funding led to an initial dearth of movies. In spite of this, in 1991 a Cannes Film Festival prize was awarded to Lebanese movie director Maroun Bagdadi for *Hors la Vie* (Out of Life). In 1998 *West Beirut*, directed by Ziad Doueiri, won international and local acclaim for the story about a teenager living in West Beirut during the first year of the civil war. In the same year, a documentary about life in the Shatila refugee camp, *Children of Shatila*, by Mai Masri, was nominated for the Amnesty International Award.

Hanan al-Shaykh is one of Lebanon's most important authors.

Caramel, a 2007 film directed by rising star Nadine Labaki, broke cultural rules in depicting the intimate relationships and conversations between five Lebanese women who work in and frequent a beauty salon in Beirut. Labaki's second work as a director, *Where Do We Go Now?*, tells the poignant story of a small, isolated Lebanese village inhabited by both Christians and Muslims at the onset of the civil war. This film won wide critical acclaim, including being selected to represent Lebanon at the Academy Awards. It won the People's Choice Award at the Toronto International Film Festival in 2011.

LITERATURE

During the civil war, Lebanese literature flourished—particularly literature written by women. A group of influential novelists, including Hanan al-Shaykh and Hoda Barakat, revolutionized Lebanese literature in its frank and devastating discussions of the effects of war on women. Called the "Beirut Decentrists" by literary critic Miriam Cooke, these women wrote influential novels that were translated into English and read around the globe, including al-Shaykh's *Beirut Blues* and Barakat's *The Stone of Laughter*.

Neither al-Shaykh nor Barakat can escape the impact of the civil war that tore apart their country for so long. But neither examines only the conflicting

Artist and writer Rabih Alameddine was born in Jordan to Lebanese Druze parents. As a teenager, he moved to California, where he pursued a career first in engineering and then in fine art. Alameddine changed careers in 1998 when he published his first novel, Koolaids: The Art of War, *that compares the devastation of AIDS in the United States during the 1980s with the Lebanese civil war. His* Hakawati *also gained critical acclaim for its retelling of the famous* 1001 Nights *through a melding of mythology and contemporary Lebanese family life.*

In 2014, Alameddine was chosen as a finalist for the National Book Award for An Unnecessary Woman, *which tells the story of a single, older Lebanese woman who secretly translates hundreds of books and hides them in her apartment as she tries to come to terms with the devastation she has experienced in her life during the wars in Lebanon.*

loyalties that drove their countrymen to kill each other. Politics, in the narrow sense of religious and nationalist causes, is of less interest to the novelists than the human landscape revealed by the war. Barakat's novel especially examines matters of gender. *The Stone of Laughter* has a male central character who, as the war proceeds, is sucked into a macho world that eventually leads him to reject his own feminine elements. Some other Lebanese works include Emily Nasrallah's *Flight Against Time*, *Sitt Marie Rose* by Etel Adnan, and *Unreal City* by Tony Hanania.

Nour Salman is a Lebanese poet who reflects on the bitter legacy of fifteen years of civil conflict that witnessed the breakdown of community life. During periods of intense fighting in the cities, the people of Beirut were always aware of the dangers of falling victim to the fighting. They felt like hostages in their own city so that, as Salman expressed it, "We are the inhabitants of the cages." Similar themes are also voiced by such other poets as Khalil Hain and Nadeen Nainy.

THE STORY OF ZAHRA

Published in 1994, Hanan al-Shaykh's The Story of Zahra *combined scenes of war-torn Beirut during the civil war with a frank discussion of women's sexuality. Zahra, the main character, descends into madness as her country descends into civil war and as she is abused by the men in her life. Finally, she falls in love with a young sniper who shoots at innocent passersby on her street. When she finds she is pregnant with his child, she excitedly tells him her plans for the future. However, as al-Shaykh suggests, there can be no future for young women in the shadow of the war's violence.*

Other important Lebanese writers include poets Kahlil Gibran, Charles Corm, and Hector Klat; novelists Amin Maalouf and Layla Balabakki; political writers Charles Malik and Antoine Najim; and playwright Elias Khoury.

ZAJAL *Zajal* (ZAH-jal) is the traditional reciting of poetry in local dialects. It is practiced across the Arab world but remains particularly popular in Lebanon. Its roots can be traced back to at least the twelfth century. The poetry often takes the form of debates between multiple poets who improvise their lines and take part in witty banter. It is typically sung to the accompaniment of percussion and sometimes a background chorus. Zajal is still performed as part of village festivals and celebratory events.

INTERNET LINKS

http://www.beirutnationalmuseum.com
This is the official website of the National Museum of Beirut.

http://www.youtube.com/user/Nancyajramworld
Nancy Ajram is a Lebanese singer and one of the most famous and adored musicians in the Arab world. You can listen to her music here, on her YouTube channel.

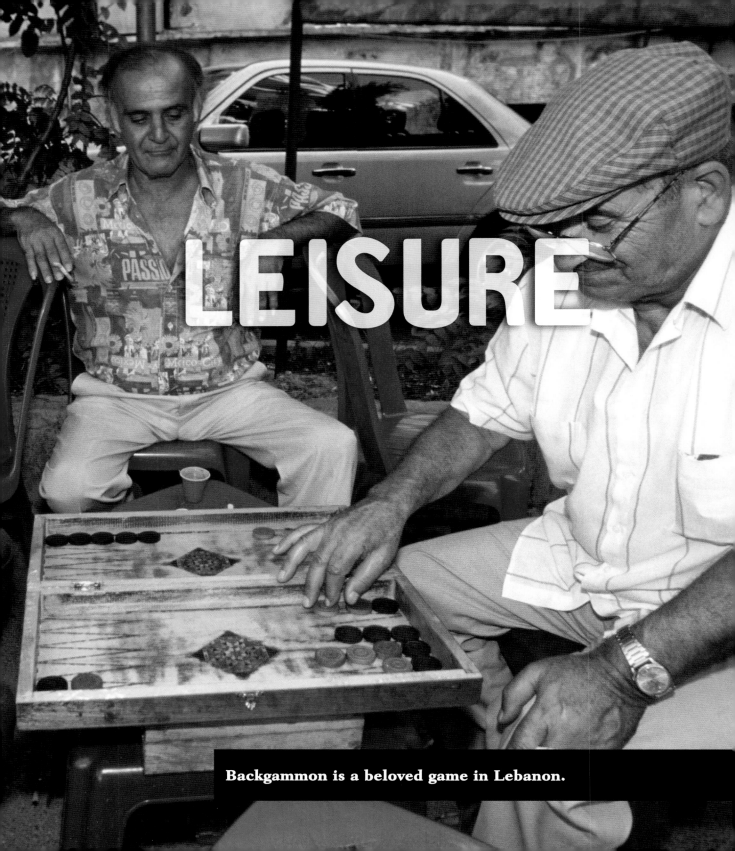

LEISURE

Backgammon is a beloved game in Lebanon.

11

S OCIAL LIFE IN LEBANON IS UNIQUE since it blends the social mores of southern European and Arab cultures. Family life is of the utmost importance to the Lebanese, and much leisure time revolves around the family unit. While parents tend to discipline their children severely, young Lebanese in Beirut have more freedom than in other Arab capitals to go out with the opposite (or same) sex and experience the nightlife the city has to offer.

FAMILY LIFE

Many Lebanese homes are not organized around the nuclear family—the mother, father, and children—as in the United States, but rather are organized around the extended family. It is not abnormal for grandparents to live with one of their children and his or her family. Oftentimes, during the holidays or other festive occasions, the whole family will get together, enlarging the already large group. However, it has become even more common for younger generations to travel abroad, particularly to countries like France, to work or to study.

THE IMPORTANCE OF CIVILITY

Civility has been refined to an art in Lebanon. When people congregate to socialize, even in an informal situation, they often begin the encounter with a number of greetings. This may not seem very different from social encounters in the West, but in practice, it is more prolonged and formal. Various greetings are made, followed by a reciprocal response to each, with slight variations in the words according to the genders of the participants. Mutual inquiries about health are also exchanged. This behavior reflects the importance attached to civility in Middle Eastern culture.

A common exchange begins with "As salaamu alaykum" (as-sah-LAHM-u ah-LAY-koom), which means "Peace be with you." The usual response is "Wa alaykum as-salaam" (wah a-LAY-koom ah-sah-LAHM), or "And upon you be peace."

Partly due to the disruption caused by the years of fighting, and partly because Lebanese people have a long tradition of traveling abroad for work and study, it is difficult for families to get together. In recent years, there has been a continuous migration of people from the countryside to Beirut and to large cities. This has also caused many families to be separated. When there is a holiday or free time, families want to be together, and reunions become an important leisure goal for many Lebanese people, young and old.

GOING OUT

Socializing can be very different for men and women, depending on where they live in Lebanon. In cities like Beirut, it is fairly common to see mixed-gender groups socializing in restaurants, cafés, and clubs. In more rural areas, however, it is generally frowned upon for unmarried men and women to socialize outside of the home. Women do not usually visit cafés in the countryside; this is more of a "man's space," where men sip tea or coffee, suck on a *nargileh* (water pipe), and play a game of cards or backgammon while chatting.

NIGHTLIFE

During and immediately following the civil war, dance clubs and bars were shuttered in the capital. However, for the past fifteen years or so, Beirut has regained its reputation as the "party capital" of the Arab world. Young Lebanese people flock to stylish rooftop bars, trendy nightclubs, and smoky jazz clubs where they can hear an eclectic mix of European and Arab music and take in the latest fashion. Many of these clubs are welcoming to different genders and sexual orientations. It is also not uncommon to see alcoholic drinks being served in Beirut clubs, though consuming alcohol is much more restricted in other parts of the country.

The capital city of Beirut has a lively nightlife and is known as the "party capital" of the Middle East.

SPORTS

Soccer is the most popular sport in Lebanon, as it is in many countries across Europe and the Middle East. In Lebanon, soccer is called football, and the game is played throughout the country, both in urban and rural areas. The most popular and largest soccer clubs are both located in Beirut: Al-Ansar and Al-Nejmeh. Al-Ansar is in the *Guinness Book of World Records* for having won eleven consecutive league titles between 1988 and 1999. Basketball is also a popular sport in Lebanon, and the professional league is one of the top leagues in Asia.

Playgrounds and schoolyards often have basketball courts. Ping-Pong is also well liked. Swimming and such water sports as boating and water-skiing are popular in the warmer months. Paragliding, hiking, and mountain biking are popular in the mountain areas from May to October. Health-conscious people in Beirut who have little time to vacation in resorts or no money for private clubs, can be seen jogging down the Corniche, a long beachfront walkway popular with anglers and strolling families.

SKIING Lebanon's mountains are perfect for skiing, and the Lebanese have been fans of the sport since a Lebanese student returned from Switzerland with a newfound love of skiing in 1913. Today, Lebanon is home to six ski resorts that come alive between November and May each year when heavy

Skiing is a popular pastime in Lebanon, thanks to the country's numerous snow-capped mountains.

snowfall coats the mountains. The closest resort to Beirut is less than an hour's drive away. The range of altitudes and mini-climates across the small country allow skiers in the spring to go down the slopes of their favorite resort in the morning and then take a quick drive to the coast to lay on the beach or enjoy some water-skiing.

Starting in 1948 and continuing to the present day, Lebanon has sent skiers to almost every Winter Olympics. Skiing remains a favorite pastime for many living there. On a fine Sunday, it is not uncommon for ten thousand skiers to take to the slopes.

LEISURE ACTIVITIES

Like many people around the world, the Lebanese enjoy a wide range of leisure activities, from playing sports to meeting friends in restaurants and cafés, or watching their favorite programs on TV. Backgammon, called *tawleh*, holds a particularly special place in the heart of many Lebanese men. If you stroll down any street in Lebanon, it would not be surprising to see two men sitting at a table playing this ancient board game. The game is almost ritualized in Lebanon, where it is commonly found in cafés, and it is played by people looking to relax after a long day's work. Chess and card games are also popular, although they don't have the special status in Lebanese culture that backgammon does.

INTERNET LINKS

http://www.lebanontraveler.com/en/magazine/Lebanon-traveler-Backgammon-a-daily-ritual
This article examines the importance of backgammon in Lebanese daily life.

http://www.zaaourclub.com
Zaaour Club is a famous resort open year-long. It is also the closest ski resort to Beirut.

FESTIVALS

British-Lebanese singer Mika performs at the Baalbeck
International Festival in 2016.

12

MOST OF THE LARGEST AND MOST important festivals in Lebanon are religious in nature. Between Muslim and Christian festivals and holidays, a religious celebration is held in almost every month of the year. The summer is a particularly busy time for arts and music festivals, including the renowned Baalbeck International Festival held in July. It features international jazz artists who play at night among the lighted ruins of the city.

RELIGIOUS FESTIVALS

Today, most people are familiar with the Gregorian calendar, which is used around the world. This calendar divides the year into twelve months with an extra day added every four years (called a leap year). This leap day allows for the difference between the calendar year of 365 days and the actual time it takes for Earth to circle the sun, which is slightly longer. Most Christian festivals throughout the world are based on the Gregorian solar calendar, meaning that their dates are fixed. For example, Christmas is always on December 25, and All Saints' Day is always on November 1. An important exception to this is Easter.

Most Muslim festivals follow what is known as a lunar calendar, which is based on the moon's rotation around Earth. There are still

The Islamic calendar is a lunar calendar consisting of 354 or 355 days over twelve months. The first year in the Islamic calendar began in 622 CE, when the Prophet Muhammad first emigrated from the city of Mecca to Medina. The twelve months are as follows: Muharram, Safar, the first Rabi, the second Rabi, the first Jumada, the second Jumada, Rajab, Shaban, Ramadan, Shawwal, Dhu-al-Qadah, and Dhu al-Hijjah.

ISLAMIC FESTIVALS

Month	Festival
Muharram 1	New Year's Day
Muharram 10	Ashura, the anniversary of the martyr Hussein's death
Rabi 12	Birth of Muhammad in 572
Rajab 27	Night of ascent of Muhammad to heaven
Ramadan 1	Beginning of the month of fasting between sunrise and sunset
Ramadan 27	Night of Power celebrates the sending down of the Quran to Muhammad
Shawwal 1	Feast of Breaking the Fast (Eid al-Fitr), celebrating the end of Ramadan
Dhu al-Hijjah 10	Feast of the Sacrifice (Eid al-Adha)

twelve months of the year, each either twenty-nine or thirty days, but the lunar year is ten or eleven days shorter than the Gregorian solar year. As a result, Muslim festivals are not held at the same time each Gregorian year; the dates vary, moving through the calendar and completing a cycle in about thirty-three years.

RAMADAN Ramadan—the ninth month of the Islamic calendar—is an important time of year for Muslims. During this month, Muslims fast from sunrise to sunset. However, this is not a mournful time, nor a trial to be endured. Rather, it is a time of celebration and family. Fasting during the day allows for shared feasts between families and loved ones at night. In Lebanon, Ramadan nights are lively and joyous, with most restaurants staying open all hours of the night and people staying up all night and then sleeping from sunrise to the late afternoon.

EID AL-FITR Eid al-Fitr, meaning "the festival of fast breaking," marks the end of Ramadan. It begins on the first day of the tenth month of the Islamic calendar and lasts four days. This is a time of family meals, prayer,

and forgiveness for past differences. It is forbidden to fast on Eid al-Fitr, and most Muslims wake up before dawn to get ready for the holiday by cleaning themselves and putting on their best clothes. A sweet breakfast, typically consisting of dates, is usually enjoyed before a special prayer. It is also customary to give a charitable donation to those in need before the prayer.

EID AL-ADHA Eid al-Adha is the Feast of the Sacrifice, and it commemorates Abraham's willingness to sacrifice his son at God's command. Eid al-Adha is a quieter celebration than Eid al-Fitr and marks the end of the hajj. According to custom, each family slaughters a sheep on the feast day. They keep one-third of the animal to feed themselves, while another third is given to friends and relatives. Finally, the last portion of the animal is donated to the poor.

ASHURA Ashura is a religious festival observed by both Sunnis and Shiites. Some Sunnis fast on this day, although it is not required. For Shiites, however, it is a solemn commemoration of the murder of Hussein, the Prophet Muhammad's grandson, during the first ten days of the month of Muharram.

Ashura is an important—and solemn—religious festival for Lebanese Shiites.

Hussein ibn Ali, or Hussein, the son of Ali, was the grandson of the Prophet Muhammad. After his father was passed up to become the Prophet Muhammad's successor, Hussein refused to pledge his allegiance to the new caliph. He continued to proclaim his legitimacy as the son of Ali and gained many followers. While traveling to visit followers in modern-day Iraq, Hussein and his caravan were intercepted by the caliph's army. Hussein, along with many of his family members and companions, was killed in the subsequent battle. His death became an important rallying cry for Shiite Muslims, and he is still mourned every year on Ashura.

This is a period of mourning and grief for Shiites. On the tenth day of the month, Shiites reenact the murder of Hussein and walk in a procession while beating their chests and performing self-flagellation, sometimes drawing blood. This passionate reenactment is to remind everyone watching of the community's grief following Hussein's assassination.

CHRISTIAN FESTIVALS

Christmas and Easter, the main Christian holidays of the year, are celebrated in Lebanon as they are celebrated around the world, with the addition of unique Lebanese customs.

At Christmastime, trees are decorated and presents purchased for family and friends. On December 24, midnight Mass is celebrated in most churches. Churches are packed with worshippers on December 25. It is a prime time for family reunions.

January 6 marks the Epiphany, a religious festival that commemorates the showing of the Infant Jesus to the Magi, the manifestation of the divinity of Christ at his baptism, and his first miracle at Cana. It is still a custom in some places to prepare special Epiphany cakes to mark the occasion. They are also known as finger biscuits because of their shape. A special syrup is made, consisting of sugar, lemon juice, rosewater, and orange-blossom water mixed

together and simmered until quite concentrated. The biscuits are soaked in this syrup and then fried in vegetable oil.

Easter is marked by processions. On Palm Sunday, the Sunday before Easter, families parade with their children, carrying branches of palm leaves, flowers, and candles. Easter Sunday begins at midnight with a procession of families, led by a priest, to the front door of their unlighted church. He knocks loudly, calling out for the door to be opened so that the King of Glory can enter. He is refused. He knocks and makes his demand three times before the door is opened and the lights come on.

INDEPENDENCE DAY

Lebanese Independence Day is celebrated on November 22 of each year and commemorates the end of the French mandate over Lebanon in 1943. This national holiday has a unique importance to the Lebanese, who suffered many years of civil conflict and sectarian fighting. It is a day of remembrance for all those who lost their lives to keep their country united.

Lebanese weddings are multi-day affairs. Beginning on the fourth day before the wedding, the bride traditionally walks through her village to display her trousseau, including sheets, pots, and pans. The next day, the bride celebrates with her close friends and family, typically decorating themselves with henna and removing body hair using a sugar and lemon mixture. The following day is the  *groom's special day, in which he sits on a throne and receives money from guests who come to congratulate him.*

The day of the wedding, a zaffe, *or traditional Arab marching band, greets the groom at his home with drums, horns, bagpipes, and dancers. The zaffe, along with friends and family, joyfully escorts the groom to his bride.*

Beirut is the center of Independence Day celebrations. The day is a national holiday, and there are parades through the city center. People use the public holiday to visit their families and friends, and celebratory meals are enjoyed.

THE BAALBECK FESTIVAL

The Baalbeck International Festival is one of the world's most famous music festivals. Established in 1955, it was initially begun to celebrate Lebanese culture and arts, and it is hosted among the Roman ruins in the ancient city of Baalbek during July and August. The festival quickly became the most prestigious festival in the country and attracted many international visitors, although it was closed due to safety concerns throughout the duration of the

> ## BYBLOS

Just as popular as the Baalbeck International Festival is the Byblos Festival. The small town of Byblos comes alive every summer for several weeks when musicians from all over the world come together to perform in front of eager crowds. In 2016, Kenny G., Sia, Grace Jones, Maxime Le Forestier, and other artists performed in various venues all over the town. The festival is known for bringing a diverse group of musicians from all around the world to share their music with festivalgoers.

civil war. From 1975 until 1996, the Baalbeck Festival was discontinued, but in 1997, it was revived. Since then, it has regained its status as Lebanon's most famous festival and hosts over forty thousand visitors each year.

Lebanese folk dances—especially the dabke, with its themes based on stories of village life—are always featured at the festival. International symphony orchestras and ballet troupes are other regular highlights. An evening ballet performance, with the dancers silhouetted against the temple ruins, is a popular event.

INTERNET LINKS

http://islam.about.com/od/otherdays/a/ashura.htm
This About Religion page explores the difference between the way Sunnis and Shiites celebrate Ashura.

http://baalbeck.org.lb
The official site of the Baalbeck International Festival provides information about the festival, as well as past and current programs.

FOOD

A table is set with traditional Lebanese mezze, including tabbouleh.

13

LEBANESE CUISINE IS OFTEN HELD UP as a gold standard across the world for delicious food. Fresh ingredients, mint, garlic, and other spices are combined to create stunning flavors. Many well-known Middle Eastern dishes are actually Lebanese in origin, including tabbouleh (cracked wheat salad), hummus (blended chickpeas), and baba ghanouj (blended eggplant). Other common ingredients include lamb, chicken, rice, yogurt, garlic, mint, lemon, and olive oil.

FAMOUS DISHES

While there are many famous Lebanese dishes, perhaps three in particular lay claim to the most popular dishes served in the country: falafel, hummus, and *fuul* (FU-ul).

Falafel is a dish of deep-fried balls of chickpea paste mixed with spices and pickled vegetables or tomatoes. It is usually eaten as a sandwich made with unleavened bread. The meat equivalent of the sandwich is shawarma (shah-WAHR-mah). Food stalls serving these are often found on city sidewalks. The meat for shawarma is sliced off a vertical spit and then squeezed into the bread and covered to overflowing with pickled vegetables or tomatoes.

Hummus, like falafel, uses chickpeas ground into a paste, but this dish is mixed with lemon, sesame oil, and garlic. It is not as spicy as falafel. Fuul, a paste made from fava beans, garlic, and lemon, is often eaten with the oil used to cook it.

Another very popular dish, which could lay claim to being the national dish, is *kibbe*, sometimes also spelled kibbeh or kibbih. It is usually made from balls of ground lamb and cracked wheat, which are often stuffed with more meat before being deep-fried with onions.

MEALS

Lebanese formal meals can contain many different courses and dishes, particularly because it is uncommon in Lebanon to drink without an appetizer nearby. Called *mezze*, these small dishes accompany drinks before the main meal. Popular mezze include a salad, such as tabbouleh, a delicious mixture of chopped onions, parsley, cracked wheat, tomatoes, lemon juice, and olive oil, as well as dips and pita bread. Common dips include hummus; *lebni* (LEB-nee), which is a thick yogurt dip mixed with lemon and garlic; and baba ghanouj, which is made of eggplant and tahini. Other popular mezze include mashed beans; spicy meatballs; *dolmas*, which are small

Tabbouleh, meat pies, and figs decorate this table.

parcels of rice and meat wrapped in grape leaves; hot and cold salads; seafood; and pistachios. Another common mezze dish is grilled shish kebab, or skewered cubes of spiced lamb, peppers, and onions.

A particularly savory mezze dish consists of crushed almonds, cashews, and walnuts mixed with garlic, onions, cayenne pepper, and spices. It is called *joh mahrouse* (JOH MAH-roose).

The main dish is usually lamb, which may be cooked in several ways—stewed with okra, grilled as spicy chops, cubed, and grilled on skewers—and nearly always served with rice. Lamb may also be served as *kefta*, spicy ground meat mixed with chopped parsley and onions. After lamb, chicken is the most popular meat.

The traditional accompaniment to most Lebanese meals is an unleavened bread called *khobez* (KOH-bez), usually oval-shaped and always served hot, which is found in many Arab countries. Outside the Middle East, this bread is called pita bread. It is used both as a spoon for scooping up food and as a sponge for soaking up sauce or gravy on the plate. An informal meal at lunchtime often consists of cooked ground lamb or chicken sandwiched inside a piece of khobez and flavored with onions and spices.

As a general rule, Lebanese meals are not highly structured. There is often no clear distinction between appetizers and main courses. There is certainly

ARRACK

Many kinds of wines and spirits are available in Lebanon. If one should look for a "national drink" in the vein of the Greek ouzo or the Turkish raki, then arrack is the Lebanese equivalent. Arrack came into existence around the beginning of the twentieth century when absinthe (a bitter anise-flavored liqueur popular in the 1800s) became illegal. Arrack is a potent rum-like brew flavored with aniseed and served mixed with water and ice. Tradition dictates that the water is added before the ice to prevent the formation of "skin" on the surface of the drink.

Arrack, an acquired taste, is a great accompaniment to many Lebanese cuisines. Arrack averages about $6 a bottle for the cheaper varieties. Better varieties that take longer to mature, from six to ten months, are naturally more expensive. Although arrack is not known for giving drinkers hangovers, it is potent and can get one drunk rather easily. Massaya, Ksara, and Le Brun are some of the good local brands.

no traditional food code that sets out in what order particular dishes can be eaten. People like to mix and match their dishes in an informal manner.

BEVERAGES

Tea and coffee are particularly popular among the Lebanese, although they may not be as palatable to Westerners because they are prepared extremely strong. Tea is often served in small, decorated glasses and is flavored with copious amounts of both mint and sugar. This is a popular drink after meals and aids in digestion. Coffee is also served with a good dose of sugar and in smaller cups. Turkish coffee, or unfiltered coffee, is widely enjoyed and has a thick and almost muddy appearance. The grounds are allowed to settle on the bottom of the cup, and sometimes the designs into which they settle are read in fortune telling. Many non-Lebanese will hesitate drinking the last sip of this strong coffee, afraid of the mouthful of dregs that have sunk to the bottom of the cup!

Lebanese enjoy drinking an Arabic coffee too, often flavored with cardamom. It also is served in tiny cups without handles that hold little more than a mouthful. Refills, poured from a silver or brass pot, continue until the drinker signals "enough" by placing a hand over the top of the cup.

The most common alcoholic drink is arrack. When diluted with water, it turns a milky white color. Wine is also made in Lebanon and is drunk with meals by non-Muslims. In rural areas, water is the most common thirst quencher.

Dotted around the countryside, at gas stations and in village centers, are earthenware jugs known as *bre* (BREE). These are filled with fresh water and made available to anyone who needs to quench his or her thirst. Other types of nonalcoholic drinks include fresh fruit and vegetable juices. *Limonada* (LIM-on-AH-DAH) is a fresh lemon drink that is popular, as is *jellab* (jell-AHB), which is made from raisins and served with pine nuts. Various yogurts are other favorite beverages.

Turkish coffee is widely enjoyed throughout Lebanon.

RESTAURANTS

Lebanese restaurants often revolve around a spit for roasting chicken or large ovens for lamb and whole fish. Lamb and other meats are often grilled over charcoal before being served, too. Oftentimes, meat is formed into kebabs by pressing spicy ground lamb onto skewers before being grilled. Kebabs are usually served with bread and a salad.

In the city, on the sidewalks or by the roadside, makeshift tables on wheels are found. Each offers some "fast" food that Lebanese stop to buy and savor on the spot to subdue hunger pangs between meals. Breads, falafel, or simply chickpeas flavored with lemon and spices, together with some squares of paper to serve as plates for these ingredients, are all the entrepreneur needs to set up a business.

KITCHENS

In rural areas, Lebanese cooks prepare their food on a wood stove. Oftentimes, the famous Lebanese flatbreads are made at home. First the dough is prepared and left out to rise. Then, it is either cooked on top of a

DESSERTS

Many people around the world know of a favorite Lebanese dessert called baqlawa *(BAHK-lah-vah), a light flaky pastry filled with honey and chopped nuts and drenched in rose-flavored syrup. But there are many other Lebanese sweets too, including* meghli *(MEGH-li), a rice pudding spiced with anise, cinnamon, and caraway seeds, and often topped with shredded coconut and nuts. Meghli is typically enjoyed for births and on Christmas.*

convex metal dome over a wood-fed fire or it is taken to the village bakery. Each rural village typically has a communal oven, called a *furn*, and residents can bring their bread to be baked there by the village baker for a small fee. This is a tradition that goes back thousands of years. Of course, life in the city is very different. Urban kitchens resemble Western ones, with the typical modern equipment. However, cities also have communal ovens where local residents can bring their bread to bake.

INTERNET LINKS

http://www.mamaslebanesekitchen.com
Mama's Lebanese Kitchen is a site that is dedicated to Lebanese recipes.

http://www.saveur.com/tags/middle-eastern-recipes
Saveur's page dedicated to Middle Eastern recipes features mostly Lebanese recipes as well as instructional articles on what spices and other ingredients to buy or common cooking techniques.

TABBOULEH

½ cup fine bulgur wheat
3 tablespoons olive oil
1 cup boiling water
2 cups finely chopped parsley
½ cup finely chopped mint
2 tomatoes, chopped
½ cucumber, peeled, cored, and chopped
3 tablespoons lemon juice
¾ teaspoon salt

Stir bulgur with 1 tablespoon olive oil in glass bowl. Pour in boiling water, cover, and let sit for fifteen minutes. Drain in a sieve to remove excess liquid. Toss with remaining ingredients, including remaining 2 tablespoons of olive oil, until well mixed. Serve slightly chilled.

MEGHLI

1 cup rice flour
1¼ cups powdered sugar
1 tablespoon caraway powder
1 tablespoon cinnamon
1 tablespoon ground anise seeds
8 cups cold water
Shredded coconut, almonds, walnuts, and/or pistachios to garnish

In a large pot, combine rice flour, sugar, caraway powder, cinnamon, and ground anise seeds. Mix well. Then add in cold water and mix again. Heat over low heat and stir continually for about twenty minutes. Remove from heat and pour into individual serving dishes. Allow to cool. Once the pudding is cool, top with shredded coconut and nuts.

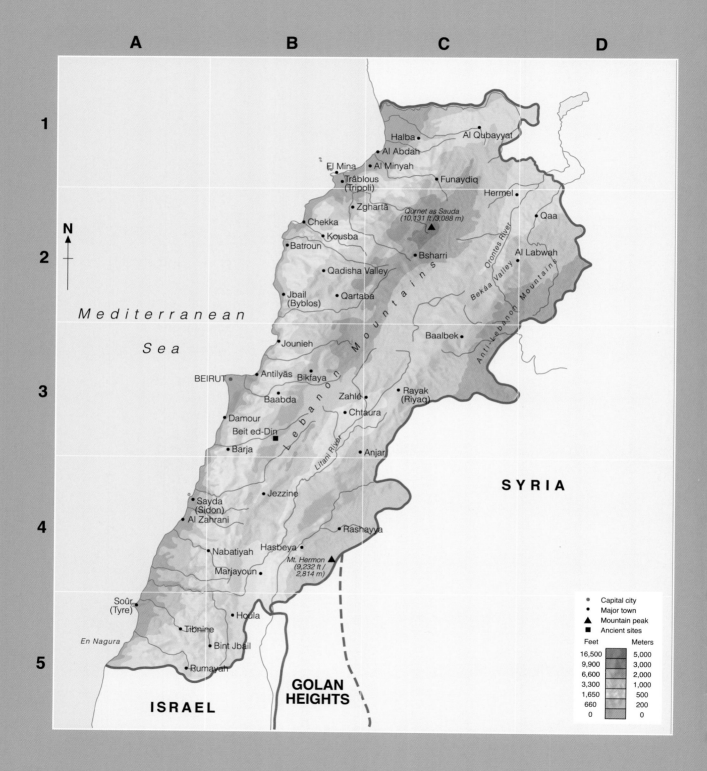

A   B   C   D

1

Halba •   • Al Qubayyat

• Al Abdah

El Mina •   • Al Minyah
• Trâblous   • Funaydiq
(Tripoli)   Hermel •

• Zghartā   Qurnet as Sauda   • Qaa
                    (10,131 ft /3,088 m)
Chekka •   ▲
          • Kousba
• Batroun   • Bsharri   • Al Labwah

2   • Qadisha Valley

Jbail •   • Qartaba
(Byblos)

Mediterranean

Sea   • Jounieh

                              • Baalbek
          • Antilyās Bikfaya
BEIRUT ●   • Rayak
          • Baabda   Zahlé •   (Riyaq)

3   • Chtaura

• Damour
Beit ed-Din ■
• Barja   • Anjar

                    SYRIA

• Jezzine

Sayda ●
(Sidon)
Al Zahrani •   • Rashayya

4
• Nabatiyah   Hasbeya •
          Mt. Hermon ▲
Marjayoun •   (9,232 ft /
                    2,814 m)

Soûr •
(Tyre)
• Tibnine   • Houla

En Nagura

5   • Bint Jbail

• Rumayah
                    **GOLAN
                    HEIGHTS**

ISRAEL

N

Orontes River
Bekáa Valley
Lebanon Mountains
Anti-Lebanon Mountains
Litani River

● Capital city
• Major town
▲ Mountain peak
■ Ancient sites

Feet   Meters
16,500   5,000
9,900   3,000
6,600   2,000
3,300   1,000
1,650   500
660   200
0   0

MAP OF LEBANON

Al Abdah, C1
Al Labwah, C2
Al Minyah, C1
Al Qubayyat, C1
Al Zahrani, A4
Anjar, B3
Anti-Lebanon
   Mountains, C3-D2
Antilyãs, B3

Baabda, B3
Baalbek, C3
Barja, B3
Batroun, B2
Beirut, B3
Beit ed-Din, B3
Bekáa Valley, C2
Bikfaya, B3
Bint Jbail, B5
Bsharri, C2

Chekka, B2
Chtaura, B3

Damour, B3

El Mina, B1
En Nagura, A5

Funaydiq, C1

Golan Heights, B5

Halba, C1
Hasbeya, B4

Hermel, C2
Houla, B5

Israel, A5-B5

Jbail, B2
Jezzine, B4

Kousba, B2

Lebanon Mountains,
   B3-C2
Litani River, B4-C3

Marjayoun, B4
Mediterranean Sea, A2
Mt. Hermon, B4

Nabatiyah, B4

Orontes River, C2

Qaa, D2
Qadisha Valley, B2
Qartaba, B2
Qurnet as Sauda, C2

Rashayya, B4
Riyaq, C3
Rumayah, A5

Sayda, A4
Sidon, A4
Soûr, A5
Syria, D4

Tibnine, A5
Trâblous, B1
Tripoli, B1
Tyre, A5

Zahlé, C3
Zghartã, B2

ECONOMIC LEBANON

Manufacturing

 Cement

 Jewelry

 Oil Refining

 Textiles

 Wood & Furniture Products

Agriculture

 Fruits & Vegetables

 Grapes

 Hemp (Hashish)

 Olives

 Sheep

 Tobacco

Natural Resources

 Limestone

 Iron Ore

 Salt

Services

 Airport

Port

 Tourism

ABOUT THE ECONOMY

OVERVIEW

After the end of the civil war, extensive borrowing from both local and foreign aid enterprises raised substantial debts that stand at nearly 170 percent of Lebanon's GDP. The Lebanese pound eventually stabilized, which led to Beirut's banks attracting billions of dollars' worth of foreign investments. Industrial production increased, and agricultural output and exports showed substantial gains. Since 2011, the Syrian civil war and the influx of Syrian refugees into the country has greatly slowed economic activity and tested government assistance, education, land use, and the environment. The banking industry, however, remains strong in spite of slow growth, and the economy remains overwhelmingly service-based, accounting for about 70 percent of its GDP.

GROSS DOMESTIC PRODUCT
$47.103 billion (2015)

CURRENCY
1 Lebanon pound (LBP) = 100 piastres
Notes: 100,000; 50,000; 20,000; 10,000; 5,000; 1,000 LBP
Coins: 500; 250; 100; 50 LBP
1 USD = 1,509.90 LBP (October 2016)

LAND USE
Arable land 11.9 percent; permanent crops 12.3 percent; others 75.8 percent (2011 estimates)

NATURAL RESOURCES
Limestone, iron ore, salt, water, arable land

AGRICULTURAL PRODUCTS
Citrus, grapes, tomatoes, figs, vegetables, potatoes, olives, tobacco, sheep, goats

MAJOR EXPORTS
Authentic jewelry, inorganic chemicals, various consumer goods, fruit, tobacco, construction minerals, electric power machinery, textile fibers, paper, hemp

MAJOR IMPORTS
Petroleum products, cars, medicinal products, clothing, meat and live animals, consumer goods, paper, textile fabrics, tobacco

MAJOR TRADING PARTNERS
United Arab Emirates, Turkey, South Africa, Switzerland, Saudi Arabia, Italy, France, Germany, China, United States, United Kingdom

INFLATION RATE
—3.8 (2015 estimate)

WORKFORCE
1.6 million (2013 estimate)

UNEMPLOYMENT RATE
6.4 percent (2014 estimate)

CULTURAL LEBANON

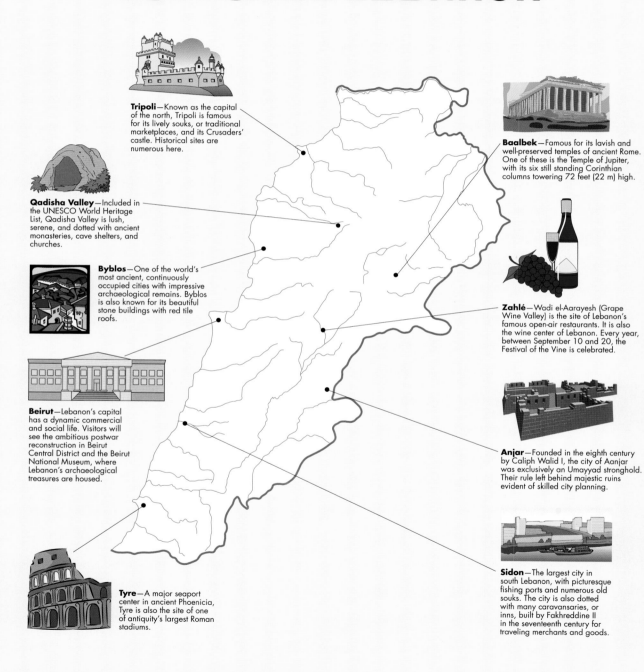

Tripoli—Known as the capital of the north, Tripoli is famous for its lively souks, or traditional marketplaces, and its Crusaders' castle. Historical sites are numerous here.

Qadisha Valley—Included in the UNESCO World Heritage List, Qadisha Valley is lush, serene, and dotted with ancient monasteries, cave shelters, and churches.

Byblos—One of the world's most ancient, continuously occupied cities with impressive archaeological remains. Byblos is also known for its beautiful stone buildings with red tile roofs.

Beirut—Lebanon's capital has a dynamic commercial and social life. Visitors will see the ambitious postwar reconstruction in Beirut Central District and the Beirut National Museum, where Lebanon's archaeological treasures are housed.

Tyre—A major seaport center in ancient Phoenicia, Tyre is also the site of one of antiquity's largest Roman stadiums.

Baalbek—Famous for its lavish and well-preserved temples of ancient Rome. One of these is the Temple of Jupiter, with its six still standing Corinthian columns towering 72 feet (22 m) high.

Zahlé—Wadi el-Aarayesh (Grape Wine Valley) is the site of Lebanon's famous open-air restaurants. It is also the wine center of Lebanon. Every year, between September 10 and 20, the Festival of the Vine is celebrated.

Anjar—Founded in the eighth century by Caliph Walid I, the city of Aanjar was exclusively an Umayyad stronghold. Their rule left behind majestic ruins evident of skilled city planning.

Sidon—The largest city in south Lebanon, with picturesque fishing ports and numerous old souks. The city is also dotted with many caravansaries, or inns, built by Fakhreddine II in the seventeenth century for traveling merchants and goods.

ABOUT THE CULTURE

OFFICIAL NAME
Al Jumhuriyah al Lubnaniyah (Lebanese Republic)

FLAG DESCRIPTION
Three horizontal bands of red (top), white (middle, with double width), and red (bottom) with a green cedar tree centered in the white band

CAPITAL
Beirut

ETHNIC GROUPS
Arab 95 percent, Armenian 4 percent, other (Assyrians, Kurds, Palestinians) 1 percent

RELIGIOUS GROUPS
Muslim (Shia, Sunni, Isma'ilite, Alawite or Nusayri) 54 percent, Christian (Catholic, Greek and Armenian Orthodox, Protestant) 40.4 percent, Druze 5.6 percent

BIRTHRATE
14.4 births per 1,000 Lebanese (2016 estimate)

DEATH RATE
4.9 deaths per 1,000 Lebanese (2016 estimate)

AGE STRUCTURE
0—14 years: 24.7 percent
15—64 years: 68.7 percent
65 years and over: 6.6 percent
(2016 estimates)

MAIN LANGUAGES
Arabic (official), French, English, Armenian

LITERACY RATE
People ages 15 and above who can read and write: 94 percent (2015 estimate)

NATIONAL HOLIDAYS
New Year's Day (January 1), Armenian Christmas (January 6), Eid al-Adha (date varies), Islamic New Year (date varies), Ashura/ Saint Maron's Day (date varies), Prophet Muhammad's Birthday (date varies), Good Friday (March/April), Orthodox Good Friday (March/April), Labor Day (May 1), Martyrs' Day (May 6), Resistance and Liberation Day (May 14), Assumption Day (August 15), Eid al-Fitr (date varies), Independence Day (November 22), Christmas Day (December 25)

LEADERS IN POLITICS
Béchara Khalil el-Khoury: first president of independent Lebanon (1943—1952)
Riyad as-Solh: first prime minister of independent Lebanon (1943—1945)
Rafiq al-Hariri: first prime minister of the new National Assembly (1992—1998)
Michel Suleiman: president from 2008 to 2014
Tammam Salam: prime minister since 2014
Michel Aoun: president since 2016

TIMELINE

IN LEBANON	IN THE WORLD
1100 BCE	
Phoenicians gain independence from Egypt.	**753 BC**
64 BCE	Rome is founded.
Phoenicians become part	**600 CE**
of the Roman Empire.	Height of Mayan civilization.
1516–1916	
Ottoman Turks conquer	**1530**
Greater Syria, which includes Lebanon,	Beginning of transatlantic slave trade organized
Syria, Jordan, and Israel.	by the Portuguese in Africa.
	1789–1799
	The French Revolution.
	1914
1918	World War I begins.
The Ottoman Empire loses to	
Britain, France, Russia, and the	
United States in World War I.	
1920	
The League of Nations grants Lebanon	
and Syria to France. The State of Greater	
Lebanon is established.	
1926	
First constitution is drafted and the	**1939**
Lebanese Republic is declared.	World War II begins.
1941	
Lebanon gains independence from France.	
1945	
Egypt, Syria, Iraq, and Lebanon form the	**1949**
League of Arab States; Lebanon becomes a	The North Atlantic Treaty Organization (NATO)
member of the United Nations.	is formed.
	1957
	The Russians launch *Sputnik 1*.
	1966–1969
1975–1990	The Chinese Cultural Revolution.
Civil war. Israel assumes control	**1986**
of south Lebanon.	Nuclear power disaster at Chernobyl in Ukraine.

IN LEBANON	IN THE WORLD
1991	**1991**
Dissolution of all militias, except Hezbollah; Lebanon signs the Treaty of Brotherhood with Syria.	Breakup of the Soviet Union.
1992	
Rafiq al-Hariri is elected as prime minister.	
1996	
Israelis bomb Hezbollah bases in southern Lebanon and a UN base, killing more than a hundred civilians.	**1997** Hong Kong is returned to China.
1998	
Émile Lahoud is sworn in as president.	
2000	
Israel withdraws troops from south Lebanon. May 25 declared "Resistance and Liberation Day."	**2001** Terrorists crash planes in New York, Washington, DC, and Pennsylvania.
2002	
Lebanon hosts the Arab League Summit.	**2003** War in Iraq begins.
2005	
Fouad Siniora is elected prime minister after Rafiq al-Hariri is assassinated.	
2008	
Lebanon establishes diplomatic relations with Syria for the first time since the 1940s.	**2011** The civil war in Syria begins.
	2013 The Islamic State (IS) captures key cities in Iraq and begins a campaign of terror.
2016	**2016**
Michel Aoun is elected president of Lebanon following former president Michel Suleiman's resignation in 2014.	IS claims responsibility for attacks in Belgium and France, among other countries.

GLOSSARY

Abbasid
Dynasty of Arab rulers that ruled Lebanon from 750 to 1250.

arrack (ah-RUCK)
The national drink, a heady liquor distilled from grapes and flavored with anise.

confession
A Lebanese community defined by religion.

Druze (Druse) (DROOS)
A Middle Eastern Muslim sect living mostly in the mountainous regions of Lebanon and Syria.

falafel (fehl-A-fehl)
Spicy, deep-fried balls of chickpea paste mixed with spices and vegetables.

Hezbollah
A radical Muslim organization that continues to oppose Israel.

hummus (HUM-us)
Chickpea paste mixed with lemon, sesame oil, and garlic.

Levant
Countries bordering the eastern shores of the Mediterranean Sea.

Maronites
Uniate Catholics. Originated in Syria in the seventh century, now chiefly found in Lebanon.

mezze **(meh-ZAY)**
Wide-ranging spread of hot and cold appetizers.

militia
A military force, especially one that is formed from the civilian population as a result of an emergency situation.

muezzin **(moo-EZ-in)**
Mosque official who calls worshippers to prayer.

oud ('ud) (OOD)
Stringed musical instrument, forerunner of the European lute.

Phoenician
A seafaring Semitic people of ancient Phoenicia, a land that included modern Lebanon.

Shiites (Shia) (SHE-ites)
An Islamic sect, originating with the murder of Ali, the Prophet Muhammad's son-in-law and nephew. The Shiites were supporters of Ali's claim to be the Islamic leader after Muhammad.

Sunni (SOO-nee)
Mainstream Islamic sect throughout the Middle East, making up 80 percent of all Muslims in the world. This group differs from Shiite Muslims in the matter of Prophet Muhammad's successor.

Umayyad (oo-MAY-ahd)
A dynasty of Arab caliphs, based in Damascus, that ruled Lebanon from 630 to 750.

FOR FURTHER INFORMATION

BOOKS

Alameddine, Rabih. *An Unnecessary Woman*. New York: Grove Press, 2014.

Fisk, Robert. *Pity the Nation: Lebanon at War*. New York: Oxford University Press, 2001.

Gibran, Kahlil. *The Prophet*. London, UK: Penguin, 2002.

Mackey, Sandra. *Lebanon: A House Divided*. New York: W. W. Norton & Company, 2013.

Marston, Elsa. *Figs and Fate: Stories About Growing Up in the Arab World Today*. New York: George Braziller, 2005.

Milligan, Max. *The Lebanon*. London, UK: Gardeners Books, 2010.

Salloukh, Bassel, et al. *The Politics of Sectarianism in Postwar Lebanon*. London, UK: Pluto Books, 2015.

Shaykh, Hanan al-. *The Story of Zahra*. Translated by Catherine Cobham. New York: Anchor Books, 1996.

WEBSITES

Beirut Times. http://www.beiruttimes.com

Central Intelligence Agency World Factbook (select Lebanon from country list). https://www.cia.gov/library/publications/resources/the-world-factbook/index.html

GreenLine. http://greenline.me.uk

Lonely Planet Guide: Lebanon. https://www.lonelyplanet.com/lebanon

Traditional Arab Music: Lebanese Music. http://www.traditionalarabicmusic.com/music_of_lebanon.html

FILMS

Caramel. Les films des tournelles, 2007.

Children of Shatila. Arab Film Distribution, 1998.

Destination: The Middle East. Pilot Film Productions, 2003.

60 Minutes: "The New Beirut." CBS, 2006.

Where Do We Go Now? Les films des tournelles, 2011.

MUSIC

Fayrouz: Live in Dubai. Enja, 2008

BIBLIOGRAPHY

Al-Monitor. http://www.al-monitor.com.

Arizona Daily Star Online. http://www.dailystar.com.

Central Administration for Statistics. http://www.cas.gov.org.

Cleary, Thomas, trans. *The Essential Koran*. San Francisco, CA: Harper, 1994.

Embassy of Lebanon. http://www.lebanonembassy.org.

Foster, Leila Merrell. *Enchantment of the World: Lebanon*. Chicago: Children's Press, 1992.

Frenea, Elizabeth and Robert. *The Arab World: Personal Encounters*. Garden City, NY: Anchor, 1985.

Lebanese Center for Policy Studies (LCPS). http://www.lcps-lebanon.org.

Lebanon in Pictures. Visual Geography Series. Minneapolis, MN: Lerner Publications, 1988.

Maalouf, Amin. *The Crusades Through Arab Eyes*. New York: Schocken Books, 1987.

Marston, Elsa. *Lebanon: New Light in an Ancient Land*. New York: Dillon Press, 1994.

Mathieson, Emily. "Interview with Mai Masri." https://www.theguardian.com/travel/2015/oct/16/mai-masri-filmmaker-beirut-lebanon-middle-east.

Musallam, Basim. *The Arabs: A Living History*. London, UK: Collins/Harvill, 1983.

United Nations. http://www.un.org.

INDEX

INDEX